Lucifer EXPOSED

THE DEVIL'S PLAN TO DESTROY YOUR LIFE

LUCIFER EXPOSED:
THE DEVIL'S PLAN TO DESTROY YOUR LIFE

© 1986 by Derek Prince Ministries-International
This edition published by Derek Prince Ministries-UK 2016
All rights reserved

ISBN: 978-1-78263-334-1
ePub: 978-1-78263-336-5
Kindle: 978-1-78263-335-8
Product code: B66EN3

Derek Prince Ministries
www.derekprince.com

Lucifer EXPOSED

THE DEVIL'S PLAN TO DESTROY YOUR LIFE

DEREK PRINCE

Contents

1

OUR INVISIBLE ENEMIES

O foolish Galatians! Who has bewitched
you that you should not obey the truth?
—Galatians 3:1

In 1963, the first year I was in the United States, I was invited to become pastor of a Pentecostal congregation in Seattle, Washington. I was a bit naive in those days and unaccustomed to many of the things that go on in American Church life. The invitation said that all twelve members of the board had unanimously agreed to invite me. So my wife, Lydia, and I packed up our belongings and took the journey to Seattle from Minneapolis (where we lived at the time).

When we arrived in Seattle, I discovered that the twelve members of the board were the only people left who still attended on Sundays!

Furthermore, after just one month, all of them had resigned except one. My wife and I found ourselves in the midst of an extraordinary situation. This congregation had been filled with a couple hundred very good Pentecostals, baptized in the Spirit. They wanted to do right; they were not a bunch of wicked backsliders. As I met them, they were very respectful toward me. But it was like they were dazed. It didn't matter what I did or said; there was no real response. It was a baffling situation.

Lydia was a tremendous woman of prayer. Together we prayed, "God, You've got to show us what's wrong with these people." The Lord clearly directed me to Galatians 3:1. "*Who has bewitched you?*" Reading that passage really challenged my theology. I thought, Pentecostals? Tongue speaking, water-baptized believers—bewitched? This called for further investigation.

I found out that the wife of the previous pastor had fallen in love with one of the board members, and he with her. They then engineered a scheme by which the wife divorced the pastor. The board member divorced his wife, and the pastor's wife married the board member. The pastor, now her former husband, moved out of the area and, unfortunately, fell away from the faith. His ex-wife became, in effect, the new pastor of the church—until I arrived. This woman seemed to control the congregation just with her eyes. I was told afterwards that every time there was an issue in the church, she would say, "Now, how many of you are for me? Put your hand up." Anybody that didn't raise their hand got one of her penetrating stares. She had them mesmerized.

Once we had identified the problem, we immediately knew that we were to enter into prayer. As a result, some wonderful things happened in that congregation. But that experience opened a whole new dimension of the spirit realm to me in a very personal way. When Paul said, "*Who has bewitched you?*" he wasn't just using a figure of speech. Paul was talking about spiritual reality.

Invisible Enemies

It is a very dangerous situation to have powerful and active enemies working against you and not even be aware that you have those enemies. As Christians, the enemies we face are not persons of flesh and blood; they are invisible spirit beings. The themes we are going to deal with in this book concern matters that are not discerned by human senses. The Bible speaks about things that "*eye has not seen, nor ear heard, nor have entered into the heart of man*" (1 Corinthians 2:9). These things are invisible and spiritual. They are only understood through the Scriptures. There is no other source of reliable information.

A lot of people imagine that what we see, touch, hear, and taste are the only truly real items. Down through the ages, however, philosophers have come to the conclusion that what we see, touch, hear, and taste are not truly real; they are temporary, and they are very often deceptive. These philosophers have warned us that you cannot rely only on your senses.

And the Bible agrees! Paul said that the things that are seen are fleeting; the things that are not seen are eternal. In other words, our sensory world is passing away, and therefore only partly real because it does not endure. (See 2 Corinthians 4:18.) But the spiritual world that we cannot see, that we cannot perceive with our senses, is the true reality. It alone will endure.

So, when we come to the theme of invisible enemies, we have to begin by making a mental adjustment. We have to say to ourselves, "I'm not going to limit myself only to the things that I can see and touch and hear and taste; I'm going to open my heart and mind to the revelation that's recorded in Scripture through the Holy Spirit, and to those things that are of a different world."

Paul prayed that God would give the Ephesian Christians a spirit of wisdom and revelation in the knowledge of Him. (See Ephesians 1:17.) I pray the same for us: that God may grant us wisdom and revelation as we open our hearts to His Word, because we are dealing with matters that are made known only through revelation.

What we are going to deal with, in essence, are two opposing kingdoms at war with one another. But they are not natural kingdoms such as Britain or Sweden or the United States. They are invisible spiritual kingdoms. One is the kingdom of God and the other is the kingdom of Satan.

The Morning Star

In Isaiah 14, we are introduced to a being called Lucifer. In its Latin root, the word Lucifer means "the one who brings light." In Hebrew, the word is translated as "the morning star." In any language, Lucifer was portrayed as a radiant, shining, and glorious being. I believe he was what is referred to as an archangel. The word *arch*, from its Greek root, means "ruling." The same word occurs in the word archbishop, a bishop who rules other bishops. Thus, an archangel is an angel who rules other angels. So, Lucifer was one of the main archangels, along with Michael and Gabriel[1], in

1 Biblical references to the archangel Michael: Daniel 10:13, 21; 21:1; Jude 9; Revelation 12:7. Biblical references to the archangel Gabriel: Daniel 8:16; 9:21; Luke 1:19-26.

God's heavenly hosts.

At some point, however, Lucifer made a grave error. He became so taken with his own glory that he sought to make himself equal with God and turned in rebellion against his Creator. It is very interesting at this point to compare Lucifer's rebellion with Jesus' obedience. Lucifer was a created being, not equal with God, who sought equality with God and fell. Concerning Jesus, Philippians 2 states, *"Who, being in very nature God, did not consider equality with God something to be grasped"* (verse 6 NIV). Jesus was equal to God, humbled Himself, and was ultimately lifted up. Returning to Isaiah, we see the motivation for Lucifer's rebellion.

> *How you are fallen from heaven, O Lucifer, son of the morning! How you are cut down to the ground, you who weakened the nations!* (Isaiah 14:12)

Notice how the phrase *"I will"* occurs five times in the next two verses. It exemplifies the will of the creature set up against the will of God.

> *For you have said in your heart: "I will ascend into heaven, I will exalt my throne above the stars of God; I will also sit on*

the mount of the congregation on the farthest sides of the north; I will ascend above the heights of the clouds, I will be like the Most High."   (Isaiah 14:13–14)

Lucifer's ambition was to elevate himself to a position of equality with God. He considered himself so wise, so beautiful, and so glorious that he apparently thought to himself: "I could be God". Scripture suggests that Lucifer undermined the loyalty of one-third of God's angels and drew them with him into his rebellion and into his fall. In response, God said, "*Yet thou shalt be brought down to hell, to the sides of the pit*" (Isaiah 14:15 KJV).

In Ezekiel 28, we get another picture of this same notorious being. The chapter is divided into two sections, each a lamentation or pronouncement of woe. The first section centers on the prince of Tyre; the second is about the king of Tyre. On closer examination, we know that the prince of Tyre was a human being. It is clearly stated that he was a man—even though he claimed to be a god. On the other hand, it is equally obvious that the king of Tyre was no human being. In this chapter, we are given a glimpse into just how Satan operates. We have a human ruler, the prince of Tyre, and behind him, in the unseen realm, we have the satanic ruler, the king of Tyre. The human ruler is not much more than a puppet who performs as the strings from the unseen realm dictate his moves. When you begin to see this truth, history and politics take on a very different meaning. As we examine many of the so-called great and infamous men of history, we begin to see evidence of the strings that guided their movements.

You were the seal of perfection, full of wisdom and perfect in beauty. You were in Eden, the garden of God; every precious stone was your covering: the sardius, topaz, and diamond, beryl, onyx, and jasper, sapphire, turquoise, and emerald with gold. The workmanship of your timbrels and pipes was prepared for you on the day you were created.

(Ezekiel 28:12–13)

It is widely accepted by biblical scholars that Lucifer was responsible for orchestrating the worship of heaven. He was a musical expert and continues to use music as a means of captivating people to this day.

*You were the anointed cherub who covers;
I established you; you were on the holy
mountain of God; you walked back and
forth in the midst of fiery stones. You
were perfect in your ways from the day
you were created, till iniquity was found
in you. By the abundance of your trading
you became filled with violence within,
and you sinned; therefore I cast you as a
profane thing out of the mountain of God;
and I destroyed you, O covering cherub,
from the midst of the fiery stones.*

(Ezekiel 28:14–16)

Now let us pause for a moment to examine
a fascinating word that appears in this passage:
"trading". In Hebrew it means, "to go up
and down as a talebearer, as an agitator, with
secret, underhanded agitation." Today we call it
campaigning or *lobbying*. That is how Lucifer
alienated the loyalty of the angels: by going back
and forth, declaring, in effect, "Look at me. See
how beautiful and intelligent I am? Don't you
think I'd make a better ruler than God up there?
And you know, God doesn't really appreciate
you. If you'll join me, I'll give you a much higher
position in my kingdom than you have at the
present time."

Let's look at some of the uses of the word *trading* in order to see the accuracy of its description, *"You shall not go about as a talebearer among your people"* (Leviticus 19:16). This verse describes a slanderer, a person bringing false insinuations and accusations. Lucifer falsely accused God of being a despot, a tyrant who only cared for His own grandeur and glory, with no appreciation of these angels who were so faithfully serving Him.

In Proverbs 11, the same word is used again, *"A talebearer reveals secrets, but he who is of a faithful spirit conceals a matter"* (verse 13). We see a contrast— the opposite of the talebearer is the man "of a faithful spirit."

In Proverbs 20, there is another vivid instance of the same word, *"He who goes about as a talebearer reveals secrets; therefore do not associate with one who flatters with his lips"* (verse 19). The talebearer and the flatterer are very closely related to one another. In other words, Lucifer flattered these angels into believing that he would give them a much better deal than God was giving them. This is so vivid for me because I have seen this activity many times on the human level in churches and other places. And it is exactly the same person who is behind that activity all through history. Flattery and lies are Lucifer's way of doing things.

In Jeremiah 6:28 and 9:4, and Ezekiel 22:9, the word is translated *slanderer*. It is the same Hebrew word: a talebearer, a slanderer, a person who goes to and fro sowing disaffection and disloyalty by using flattery and misrepresenting authority.

Lucifer's Pride

Returning to Ezekiel 28, we see precisely what caused Lucifer's downfall.

Your heart was lifted up because of your beauty; you corrupted your wisdom for the sake of your splendor. (Ezekiel 28:17)

What was the initial motivation of Lucifer? What was the first sin? Pride. The first sin took place in heaven, not on earth. It wasn't drunkenness, it wasn't adultery, and it wasn't even lying. It was pride. And it is still the most deadly of all sins. There are scores of churchgoers who wouldn't dream of committing adultery or getting drunk but who are easily enticed into pride without realizing how dangerous it really is.

The archangel Lucifer was so beautiful he became proud. The transition from archangel

Lucifer to Satan was made complete through his pride.

> *You defiled your sanctuaries by the multitude of your iniquities, by the iniquity of your trading.*   (v. 18)

Lucifer had been responsible for the sanctuary of God in heaven. He was in charge of the worship. He was the cherub who covered the place where God's presence was manifested. He was responsible for the music. He was an artist. He was very accomplished. Then he rebelled and he fell. Pride!

2

THE BATTLE LINES ARE DRAWN

Now Satan stood up against Israel.
—1 Chronicles 21:1

Lucifer was perhaps the wisest and most beautiful of all God's creatures. But Scripture says his heart was *lifted up.* (See Ezekiel 28:2–19.) After growing proud because of his wisdom and his beauty, and after hatching his planned rebellion against God, he was cast down from the presence of God, and his traitorous angels were cast down with him.

To counteract the effects of Lucifer's rebellion, God devised an alternative plan. Since pride had been the root of Lucifer's rebellion, God's response was to make a different kind of creature—one that was destined to take Lucifer's place. The new creature God devised for this purpose was *man*. Or, as he's referred to in the Hebrew, 'adam, bearing in mind that Adam is a proper name as well as the name of our race.

God's Alternative Plan

God created Adam as unique from any other creature. There was something special about Adam's mode of creation that was designed in the mind of the Creator to militate against pride. Adam came from a source different from any other created being that we know of: the very lowest, the very humblest. Yet God made him capable of becoming the very highest. God combined in Adam both the lowest and highest. Here's the description of the creation of Adam in Genesis:

> *And the LORD God formed man* [or 'adam] *of the dust of the ground, and breathed into his nostrils the breath of life; and man became a living being* [or "soul," KJV].   (Genesis 2:7)

For me, that is such a vivid picture. And I believe it took place just the way it is described. I can see the great Creator, the one through whom all things were created as the New Testament reveals, the eternal Son of God, the Word of God, the second person of the Godhead. I see Him there in that garden, stooping down, and with His divine fingers molding a perfect figure of clay. But in the end, although it was so perfect, it was just clay. Then the Creator stooped yet lower. He placed His divine lips against those lips of clay, His divine nostrils against those nostrils of clay, and He breathed into him the breath of life.

Let me point out five vital facts about the creation of man, or Adam, as revealed in this passage. First of all, this is the first time in the record of Scripture that personal names are introduced. It says, *"The LORD God formed man* ['adam]." *"The LORD"* (in small caps) is the sacred, personal name of the true God. We usually call it Jehovah. Modern scholars say it was probably Yahweh. But here is the important thing to remember: it is a personal name.

Likewise, man *('adam)*, is a personal name. So a personal God created a personal man for a person-to-person relationship between them. This indicates that the great intent of the Creator was to have fellowship with His creature, person to person.

Second, we see that God stooped to create man. He bent in the dust and formed the body; then He stooped still lower and put His lips against those lips of clay and breathed His divine breath into that body. God had to stoop to create man.

Third, God imparted Himself to man. He breathed His very own divine breath into that body of clay.

Fourth, as a result, God combines in man the highest and the lowest—that which is from God Himself directly, and that which is from the earth, the dust. Can you understand something about yourself when you consider this? There is something very high and something very low in you. And a large part of our total experience is the conflict in each of us between the high and the low.

The fifth fact is that man now has the potential for a dual relationship with God. Through his spirit, that which came from God, man relates to God. But through his body, that which came from the earth, man relates to the world. So again we see something that is true in our experience. There is something in us that relates to God, which was made for fellowship with Him, for person-to-person relationship. But, there is also something in us that is very earthly that relates to this world.

Here we have the picture of God's alternative plan. The created cherub had fallen. So God, in order to undercut the tendency toward pride, created another kind of being from a different source—the earth—into whom He breathed His own divine life.

Satan's Counterattack

Satan, the already-fallen angel, the enemy of God and of man, retaliated. He had particular enmity against man for two reasons. First of all, he could attack God's image in man. You see, man visibly represented God to the rest of creation. Satan could not touch God Himself, but he could make war against the very image of God within man. His delight was to defile that image, to destroy it, to humiliate it—and to that end he worked tirelessly.

The second reason Satan had such malice toward man was due to the fact that man was destined to take Satan's place of dominion. From the moment of man's creation, Satan saw him as a rival whom he needed to eliminate.

Ironically, Satan procured man's downfall through the same motivation that caused his own downfall. That process is described in Genesis. In the form of the serpent, Satan came into the garden where God had placed Eve with Adam and tempted them into disobedience and rebellion. This is the record of that deception and downfall:

*Now the serpent was more crafty than any
of the wild animals the LORD had made.
He said to the woman, "Did God really
say, 'You must not eat from any tree in the
garden'?" The woman said to the serpent,
"We may eat fruit from the trees in the
garden, but God did say, 'You must not eat
fruit from the tree that is in the middle of
the garden, and you must not touch it, or
you will die.'" "You will not surely die,"
the serpent said to the woman. "For God
knows that when you eat of it your eyes
will be opened, and you will be like God,
knowing good and evil."*

(Genesis 3:1–5 NIV)

To our dismay, we are all too familiar with this
record. Eve was persuaded by the temptation of
Satan the serpent, reached out her hand, took the
fruit, and convinced her husband to join her in
disobedience.

I want to point out three specific phases of
temptation—the way that Satan came against
Adam and Eve to entice them to rebel.

Satan's first attack was directed against God's
word as He had conveyed it to Adam and Eve.
God had said to Adam, *"You must not eat from
the tree of the knowledge of good and evil, for*

when you eat of it you will surely die" (Genesis 2:17). Satan's first approach was to question God's word. He said to Eve, *"Did God really say, 'You must not eat from any tree in the garden'?"* (Genesis 3:1). Satan was too subtle to begin with a direct denial, so he began with a question. His motive was to discredit God's word. When Eve entertained the question, he then proceeded to discredit God Himself.

Next, the serpent said to the woman, *"You will not surely die....For God knows that when you eat of it your eyes will be opened, and you will be like God, knowing good and evil"* (verses 4–5). The thrust of that statement is self-evident. The implication is that God was an arbitrary tyrant who, after creating Adam and Eve, was keeping them in a position lower than what they deserved. Satan inferred that God knew they had the potential and ability to become something much higher, but He was keeping them in arbitrary and unreasonable subjection. Having first discredited God's word, Satan then proceeded to discredit God's character. He wanted to give them a false picture of their loving and gracious Creator. He wanted to paint God as an arbitrary despot by discrediting the word of God and the very character of God Himself.

In the third phase, Satan offered to Adam and Eve the very same motivation that had caused his own fall—the prospect of equality with God. He said, *"When you eat of it your eyes will be opened, and you will be like God, knowing good and evil"* (verse 5). In effect, he was saying, "You won't need to depend any longer on God. You'll have enough knowledge in yourself that you'll be equal with God." That was exactly the same temptation that impelled his fall: *"I will make myself like the Most High"* (Isaiah 14:14 NIV), he had said. Now he was saying to Adam and Eve, "You will be like God. This position of subjection and dependence that you're in isn't worthy of you. You're capable of a higher destiny. Reach up and reach out for knowledge that will set you free from this slavish dependence on your Creator."

It is very clear that Adam's sin was a carbon copy of Satan's error. Both Satan and Adam were created on a certain level—a level that was blessed, appointed, and ordained by God. But through pride, they both reached up for equality with God. And reaching up, they fell. Remember, *"Whoever exalts himself will be humbled"* (Luke 14:11).

Still Lower

How would God now respond to the fall of Adam? In creating man, God stooped to the dust, but in the transition from creation to redemption, God stooped still lower. God's answer to pride is always humility. The more God encounters pride, the more He Himself displays humility.

Man had fallen. He was alienated, a rebel. God did not abandon him. Thank God for that. In the person of Jesus Christ, God stooped to the lowest level. He identified Himself with the fallen race and expiated its guilt. Then, to crown it all, He exalted these fallen, but redeemed, creatures to the highest place in the universe, continually demonstrating an immutable principle: "The way up is down."

Let's look at some Scriptures that speak, first of all, about how Christ identified Himself with the human race and extinguished its guilt.

Since the children have flesh and blood, he too shared in their humanity so that by his death he might destroy him who holds the power of death—that is, the devil—and free those who all their lives were held in slavery by their fear of death.

(Hebrews 2:14–15 NIV)

Earlier, I pointed out that when Adam rebelled, instead of becoming a king, he became a slave— a slave of Satan, a slave of death, a slave of corruption. He was no longer free. But in order to deliver him from that slavery, Jesus took upon Himself the Adamic nature, the form of humanity. To share in humanity, He took upon Himself the same flesh and blood you and I have. The significance of this is that by His death, He would destroy the one who holds the power of death (the devil) and free all of us who were held in slavery to the fear of death.

What Jesus achieved was a total identification. In order to redeem all humans, Jesus took upon Himself the nature of man, the fallen creature. This is stated, too, in 1 Peter:

> *He himself bore our sins in his body on the tree, so that we might die to sins and live for righteousness; by his wounds you have been healed.*   (1 Peter 2:24 NIV)

On the cross, Jesus became totally identified with our sin, our guilt. He Himself became the last great guilt offering that took away the sin and guilt of the human race. He bore our sin. He bore our punishment.

Our wounds became His wounds. And He died our death. He eliminated that guilt of rebellion as our representative—the last Adam, hanging there on the cross, shedding His lifeblood, giving Himself totally to redeem us.

And then the simple statement:

For Christ died for sins once for all, the righteous for the unrighteous, to bring you to God.   (1 Peter 3:18 NAS)

That is total identification. The righteous took the place of the unrighteous, of the rebel, the alien, the one who had turned against God. He died the death that was our due, to deliver us from the fear of death and to reconcile us to God.

As we look further, beyond Christ's identification with us, we find that in turn, through faith and repentance, we can be identified with Christ—identified not only in His death, but in His subsequent exaltation. This is the great mystery of identification; first, Christ with us; then we, through faith, with Christ.

But because of his great love for us, God, who is rich in mercy, made us alive with Christ even when we were dead in transgressions—it is by grace you have been saved. And God raised us up with Christ and seated us with him in the heavenly realms in Christ Jesus.
          (Ephesians 2:4–6 NIV)

Our redemption is the other side of the coin, the opposite side of identification. First, Jesus identified Himself with us, the fallen race. He took our place. He paid our penalty. He died our death. He expiated our guilt. Then, recognizing these facts and identifying ourselves in turn with Him in faith, we are identified with Him in all that follows His death. That passage in Ephesians 2 states three great steps of our identification with Jesus: God made us alive with Christ, God raised us up, and God resurrected us with Christ. But it doesn't stop there. God seated us with Him in the heavenly realm. Christ is seated on a throne; God seated us with Him. He has enthroned us with Christ. Notice those three upward steps of our identification with Jesus: made alive with Him, resurrected with Him, and enthroned with Him. It is the same immutable principle: the way up is down. We go from the lowest to the highest.

Amazingly, God has made these redeemed creatures, who were fallen and raised up, His eternal demonstration to the whole universe that God exalts the lowest to the highest. Please don't miss the principle that runs through the story of redemption. It is not just a matter of history. It is a matter of the outworking of a universal law: Whoever humbles himself will be exalted. Whoever exalts himself will be humbled. (See again Luke 14:11.)

One Sacrifice

The sacrificial death of Jesus on the cross is the only basis of God's provision for every need of the whole human race. Instead of God doing a lot of different actions at different times, Scripture says, *"By one offering* [sacrifice] *He has perfected forever those who are being sanctified"* (Hebrews 10:14). The writer of Hebrews explained that after Jesus had offered that one sacrifice, He *"sat down at the right hand of God"* (v. 12). Why did He sit down? Because He was never going to have to do it again.

Through the cross, Jesus administered to Satan and his kingdom a total, permanent, irreversible defeat. Jesus will never have to do that work again. Satan has already been defeated. You and I do not have to defeat Satan. But we must apply the victory that Jesus has already won and walk in that victory.

Giving thanks to the Father who has qualified us to be partakers of the inheritance of the saints in the light.
(Colossians 1:12)

Our inheritance is in the light, and there is no darkness whatsoever in it. It is totally in the light.

*How has He done it? He has delivered us
from the power* [I prefer to say domain]
of darkness and conveyed [translated] *us
into the kingdom of the Son of His love,
in whom we have redemption through His
blood, the forgiveness of sins.* (vv. 13–14)

So, by redemption through the blood of Jesus
we have been delivered from the domain of
darkness and translated, or carried over, into the
kingdom of the Son of God's love.

That word that is translated *domain* or *power* is
actually the normal Greek word for "authority." In
speaking of *domain* or *power*, it is very important
for us to understand that Satan has authority.
Why does he have authority? Because he is the
ruler of all those who are in rebellion against
God. Anyone who is in rebellion against God is
automatically under the authority of Satan. He is
in the "domain of darkness."

And you [God] *made alive, who were dead
in trespasses and sins...* (Ephesians 2:1)

That is not physical death. That is spiritual
death, and it applies to all of us. That's where all
of us were. We were all dead to God because we

were living in trespasses and sins.

In which you once walked according to the course of this world, according to the prince of the power of the air.   (Verse 2)

Satan is the ruler with authority in the region of the *air.* There are two Greek words for air. One of them gives us the English word *ether.* The other gives us the English word *air.* The difference in Greek is as follows: *ether* is the higher, rarer atmosphere; *aer* (*air* in English) is the lower atmosphere, contiguous with the earth's surface. The word used here has the second meaning. Satan is the ruler of the realm of authority of the surface of the earth, contiguous with the earth. The passage in Ephesians states that he is: .

..the spirit who now works in the sons of disobedience.   (v. 2)

Why does he work in those people? Because they are disobedient to God. We have only two options: we can either be in Satan's territory or in God's territory. There is no third option.

If we are submitted to God's appointed ruler, Jesus, we have the right to be in God's kingdom. If we have rejected or not accepted God's appointed ruler, Jesus, we are in Satan's kingdom because we are sons of disobedience. Satan has legitimate authority over all those who are in rebellion against God. Whether they speak in tongues or not is unimportant. Satan rules over all rebels.

Among whom also we all once conducted ourselves in the lusts of our flesh, fulfilling the desires of the flesh and of the mind.

(v. 3)

"We *all*" did this. All of us. Notice also that our errors were not just the flesh. Our minds also were alienated from God. Scripture says the carnal mind is enmity toward God. (See Romans 8:7.) You have an enemy of God dwelling in your cranium, the carnal mind.

Continuing in Ephesians 2, we read:

[We] *were by nature children of wrath, just as the others.*   (v. 3)

That is a very important statement. We were born with a disobedient nature. This is a fact of human experience. How many parents ever had to train their children to be naughty? Not one, because in every descendant of Adam, there is the nature of a rebel. Adam never had any children until he was a rebel. Consequently, everyone who descended from Adam has inherited the nature of a rebel. That nature makes us subject to the authority of Satan.

The Way Out

God offers a way out of Satan's kingdom and into God's kingdom. This is so vivid for me. Some years ago while I was preaching in the country of Zambia, I was in a remote area in the west of the country, right on the border of the Zambezi River, which at that point separates Zambia from Zaire. I had a congregation of about four or five hundred Africans, and I was trying to communicate to them this wonderful fact that God has made it possible for us to escape from the kingdom of Satan and get into the kingdom of God. I said to them, "Suppose here on the east side of the Zambezi River we were in the kingdom of darkness. But on the other side of the river is the kingdom of light. In order to get from the kingdom of darkness into the kingdom of light, we need to have a bridge across the river." I said, "God has provided a bridge. There is only one bridge—the cross of Jesus Christ. By taking that bridge you can cross out of the kingdom of darkness into the kingdom of the Son of God's love."

God doesn't simply want us to stay on the bridge. He wants us to get into another kingdom and rule with Jesus now as kings and priests. That is our destination. Here is the problem with the Christian Church—we have millions and millions of people who have gotten out of the kingdom of darkness but they are still hanging around on the bridge. They have never moved over into the kingdom of God. Lots of people say, "I'm saved, and that's it." It's wonderful to be saved, but that is not the end. The bridge is just the way from one kingdom to another kingdom. The New Testament teaches that through redemption by the blood of Jesus, God has made us kings and priests in the here and now.

Those who receive abundance of grace and of the gift of righteousness will reign in life now through the One, Jesus Christ.
(Romans 5:17)

Let me ask you a direct question: Where are you right now? Are you hanging around on the bridge? Or are you reigning in life with Jesus? Everyone believes they will reign in the next life. That is wonderful, but it is not what God is concerned about right now. He is concerned about where we are in this life.

What Did Jesus Accomplish?

It is very important for us to see how Jesus accomplished what He accomplished.

Having disarmed principalities and powers, He [Jesus] *made a public spectacle of them, triumphing over them in it.* (Colossians 2:15)

What principalities and powers did He disarm through the cross? Who is represented by the word *them*? That's right, Satan and his minions. Other translations identify "rulers and authorities" (NAS, for example) as the ones Jesus disarmed on the cross.

For we do not wrestle against flesh and blood, but against principalities, against powers [notice the same words as in Colossians 2:15], *against the rulers of the darkness of this age, against spiritual hosts of wickedness in the heavenly places.* (Ephesians 6:12)

I am privileged to have studied Greek since I was ten years old. (Actually, it wasn't always a privilege, believe me!) But I am qualified to teach it at the university level. That doesn't mean I am always right, but at least I am entitled to my informed opinion. (In actuality, nobody is always right about the Greek language; it is historically a very complicated language.) But I will offer you the "Prince version" of the verse that talks about wrestling against flesh and blood: "For our wrestling match is not against persons with bodies."

We are not fighting persons with bodies. We are in a wrestling match with a very powerful and highly organized kingdom, which has rulers, sub-rulers, and sub-sub-rulers. Each ruler is responsible to Satan for a certain area under his authority. Satan has the whole world divided up into areas that he seeks to dominate through these rulers. To continue the "Prince version" of Ephesians 6:12: "...against the world dominators of this present darkness."

I deliberately use the word *dominators* here because the Greek word is very strong, and because domination is characteristically a satanic activity. God never dominates, so if you meet domination, you can be sure you're not dealing with God. I refer to the powers we deal with as "the world dominators of this present darkness." Satan's aim, which he is steadily and consistently pursuing, is to become the ruler of this world. One place we see this clearly is in reference to the end times. As I understand prophecy pertaining to that time, there will be a very short period right at the end of the age when Satan will temporarily succeed. He will do so through a certain man whom he will raise up, called the Antichrist, one who will be empowered by Satan. Satan will persuade much of the world (those whose names are not written in the Lamb's Book of Life) to worship the Antichrist. In worshiping him, they will actually be worshiping Satan who empowered him.

Why does Satan want above all things to be worshiped? It relates to his desire to be equal with God, which was the cause of his fall. Today, Satan is not on the level he experienced before his fall, but he still has one way to claim equality with God—through worship. That is the one activity that belongs by right only to God. But if Satan can receive worship, it affirms his claim to be equal with God. When we become truly aware of the conflict of kingdoms, we find that Satan's supreme ambition is to be worshiped. It is also very important to realize that what we worship is what has power over us. I have dealt with people who have worshiped Satan. Believe me, to get them free is a major battle because Satan feels he has legitimate power over them.

The final description of this satanic kingdom in Ephesians 6:12 is *"spiritual hosts* [or forces] *of wickedness in the heavenly places."* Satan's headquarters are not in hell; they are in the heavenlies. Some of the traditional language in the Church does not correspond with Scripture on this matter. To people who say Satan is in hell, I reply, "It would be nice if it were true, but it isn't." Satan is very much at large. Peter wrote this warning: *"The devil walks about like a roaring lion, seeking whom he may devour"* (1 Peter 5:8).

Let us now examine the fact that Jesus disarmed the principalities and powers of Satan. He stripped them of all their weapons. The Greek is very emphatic. He left them nothing. How did He do it?

Removing the Barrier

First, we need to understand that Satan's number one weapon against the human race is *guilt*. Jesus stripped him of the ability to make us guilty. Let's examine the facts that we know. God had already dealt with Satan before

He created Adam. Satan was already a fallen angel, the enemy of God and anything that God created—particularly man. Satan then succeeded in tempting Adam into the same rebellion that he had chosen. In his temptation Satan said, "You shall be like God," which was exactly what had first motivated his own fall.

Let us assume that Satan knows a lot about God's feelings and attitudes and he knows of God's love for the human race. We read in the book of Job that when the angels came to appear before God, Satan came amongst them. (See Job 1:6.) At that time, he still had some access to the presence of God. Furthermore, the text seems to indicate the only person who spotted Satan was the Lord, because he had transformed himself into an angel of light.

I imagine the dialogue between Satan and God might have gone like this:

Satan says to the Lord, "You're a righteous God. You're a just God, and I'm a rebel. I know it. I've got no doubt about it. See that lake of fire over there with all the unpleasant smoke coming out of it? I know that's where I'm headed. I know it was created for me and for my angels. But God, I just want to remind You of something. You see these men and women that You love? They're as guilty as I am. They're rebels too. So when You throw me and my angels into that lake, You're going to have to throw them into that lake. Just remember, God, Your justice makes it essential."

I suppose we might imagine that for centuries God didn't answer Satan. But God had His plan. His plan was Jesus. And when Jesus came, He became the last Adam, the final representative of the Adamic race. He took upon Himself all the guilt and all the condemnation and all the evil consequences of Adam's transgression. He died as "the last Adam," He was buried as "the last Adam," and He rose again as "the second man," the head of a new race. In that way, Jesus extinguished the guilt of Adam's race. For those who believe in Jesus, the guilt of Adam is no longer held against them. As a result of Jesus' sacrifice, God can now forgive us without compromising His justice. He has removed Satan's argument from him by the death of Jesus. He has made it possible for us to be received by God as righteous without any condemnation.

If we look briefly in Colossians, we will see how Jesus removed our guilt:

And you, being dead in your trespasses and the uncircumcision of your flesh, He has made alive together with Him, having forgiven you all trespasses, having wiped out the handwriting of requirements that was against us, which was contrary to us. And He has taken it out of the way, having nailed it to the cross. (Colossians 2:13–14)

Through the death of Jesus, without compromising His justice, God can forgive us all our past acts of disobedience. How many of them? All of them. If even one sin were left unforgiven, we would have no right of access to God. Thankfully, God has made it possible for us to be assured that all our past sinful acts have been forgiven.

For he himself [Jesus] *is our peace, who has made the two* [Jew and Gentile] *one and has destroyed the barrier, the dividing wall of hostility, by abolishing in his flesh the law with its commandments and regulations.*   (Ephesians 2:14–15 NIV)

Nothing could be clearer than that. He abolished the law with its commandments and regulations.

Therefore by the deeds of the law no flesh will be justified in [God's] *sight, for by the law is the knowledge of sin.*

(Romans 3:20)

We are justified. As this Scripture attests, no human being will achieve righteousness in the sight of God by keeping the law. The problem isn't with the law; the problem is with us. We can't keep it. And we can't split the law up into a lot of different sections and say, "I'll keep Section A and ignore Sections B and C. I'll keep Section D and then I'll keep a few other sections." The law is one law. You either keep it all—perfectly—all the time, or you do not achieve righteousness by it. There's no other option.

For sin shall not have dominion over you, for you are not under law but under grace.   (Romans 6:14)

Notice that law and grace are mutually exclusive alternatives. If we are under law, we can't be under grace. If we are under grace, we can't be under law. We can't have it both ways at the same time. If we are under law, sin will have dominion over us. If we are under grace, Paul said sin will not have dominion over us because we are not under law.

Living in Freedom

For as many as are led by the Spirit of God, these are sons of God.

(Romans 8:14)

How do we live as sons (and daughters) of God? By being led by the Holy Spirit. This is a vital truth that has escaped the notice of most Christians. We talk about being saved, baptized in the Spirit, baptized in water, and that's it. But that is only the entrance. Life is being led by the Spirit daily, hourly, moment by moment.

For Christ is the end of the law for righteousness to everyone who believes.
(Romans 10:4)

If we believe, then for us Christ is the end of the law for righteousness. Not the end of the law as part of God's Word. Not the end of the law as part of the history of the culture of Israel. But it is the end of the law as a means of achieving righteousness with God. This is true for everyone who believes: Jew or Gentile, Protestant or Catholic. It makes no difference. If we are reckoned righteous with God by the death of Jesus, it means the end of the law.

But if you are led by the Spirit, you are not
under the law.   (Galatians 5:18)

We can choose, but we can't have it both ways. Jesus has made it possible for us to be guiltless and not condemned. He has abolished the law as a means of achieving righteousness with God. As long as we are seeking to achieve righteousness by keeping a law, we will never be without condemnation. We can never be sure we have done enough. We can never be sure that before each day ends we will not have broken some aspect of the law.

I am not suggesting we should be lawless or disobedient. What I am saying is we will never achieve righteousness with God by keeping a set of rules. To try to do that is to insult God, because we are telling Him, in effect, "Jesus didn't need to die. I could have made it without Him." What a terrible thing to say: that the death of Jesus wasn't necessary. So, we are set free from condemnation on the basis of these two facts. First, our past sins can be totally forgiven— all of them. Second, we are not required to observe a law to achieve righteousness with God.

3

WARFARE AGAINST THE KINGDOM OF DARKNESS

---

*That you may be able to withstand in the
evil day, and having done all, to stand.*

(Ephesians 6:13)

In the matter of spiritual warfare, Christ
has clearly won the victory. However, He
leaves it to us to *enforce* that victory. It is very
important that we understand this. If we had to
win the victory, we could never do it. It is a good
thing for us that we don't have to. Jesus said, "I
have won the victory." It is our task to enforce the
victory that He has won.

We see this principle after the resurrection
when Jesus appeared to His disciples and said:

All authority in heaven and on earth has

*been given to me. Therefore go and make
disciples of all nations.*

(Matthew 28:18 NIV)

It is clear that Jesus has *obtained* the authority.
We have to *exercise* the authority. In a sense,
His authority is completely ineffective until we
exercise it. The only way the world can ever fully
understand what Jesus has accomplished is for us
to exercise His authority on His behalf, making
disciples of all nations. This is a clear scriptural
principle. Jesus has done it; we have to apply it.

There are two mistakes we must be careful not
to make. The first is thinking that we have to win
the victory. We don't have to because Jesus has
won the victory. The second mistake is thinking
there is nothing left for us to do. That is not true
either. We have to take steps to apply the victory
that Jesus has won.

The first step we must take is to put on the
whole armor of God. In Ephesians 6, where
Paul spoke about the kingdom of Satan in the
heavenlies, he immediately followed with this:

*Therefore take up the **whole** armor of God,
that you may be able to withstand in the
evil day, and having done all, to stand.*
(Ephesians 6:13, emphasis added)

Notice, we must take it up. The armor does not grow on us. Neither does God place it on us. We have to take it up. Paul was writing to people who were Christians—much like you and me—and he assigned them the responsibility to take up the armor.

Defensive Armor

First of all, let us look in 2 Corinthians, where Paul was addressing all Christians. This is not just written to apostles or pastors. It applies to all Christians.

> *For though we walk in the flesh, we do not war according to the flesh.*
>
> (2 Corinthians 10:3)

Paul said that we live in physical bodies and we are involved in a war. But the war is not in the physical realm. If, then, the war is not in the physical realm, it must be in the spiritual.

> *For the weapons of our warfare are not carnal but mighty in God for pulling down strongholds [or fortresses], casting down arguments and every high thing that*

exalts itself against the knowledge of God,
bringing every thought into captivity to
the obedience of Christ.   (vv. 4–5)

Where the *New King James Version* says
"arguments," other versions say *"reasonings"*
(Young's Literal Translation) or *"speculations"*
(NAS). We also find the words *knowledge* and
thought used in this verse. If we examine those five
words—*arguments, reasonings, speculations,
knowledge,* and *thought*—we recognize they all
belong to the same realm: the mind. This is a vital
fact. The battlefield is the mind. That is where the
battle is fought. Anyone who has tried to live the
Christian life has discovered this, I'm sure. We
may not always recognize it as a theological fact,
but the truth of the matter is clear—most of our
battles are in our mind.

Another point we must consider about our
warfare, remembering that we are all in it, is that
our kingdom is at war with Satan's kingdom. We
are citizens of the kingdom of God; therefore, we
are at war with Satan.

The Nature of Strongholds

The weapons God has given us are mighty for
pulling down strongholds or fortresses. Whose

fortresses are we pulling down? Satan's. And in what realm? The realm of the mind.

Satan builds many different fortresses in people's minds, but if I were to choose one word to sum them all up, it would be the word *prejudice*. Prejudice means having your mind made up before you know the facts. The typical statement of the prejudiced person is, "My mind is made up; don't confuse me with the facts!" In its variety of forms, prejudice is one of the most powerful strongholds of Satan. He builds prejudice as a fortress in people's minds to prevent the truth of the gospel entering and doing its work.

We see this vividly in regard to people involved in cults and false religions. A believer can quote the Bible perfectly to them, but they can't hear because their minds are totally preprogrammed. They will have a specific way to answer you. And that represents a fortress in their minds that prevents the truth of God's Word from entering.

This is clear also in encounters with Muslims. Even though they may believe certain truths about Jesus, even admitting that He was the Messiah, even agreeing He was born of a virgin, there are two things they will never admit. First, that Jesus died on the cross. Mohammed taught that an angel spirited Jesus away before He died. Second, they will passionately oppose that He is the Son of God. Those are the strongholds in the Muslim mind. And they are very powerful strongholds. A Muslim may go a long way in his interest in Jesus, but when He is asked to acknowledge that Jesus is the Son of God, a wall comes up. Only supernatural weapons can demolish that wall.

The Nature of Our Weapons

Let us now consider some of the weapons described in Ephesians:

Therefore, take up the whole armor of God, that you may be able to withstand in the evil day, and having done all, to stand. Stand therefore, having girded your waist with truth, having put on the breastplate of righteousness, and having shod your feet with the preparation of the gospel of peace; above all, taking the shield of faith with which you will be able to quench all the fiery darts of the wicked one. And take the helmet of salvation, and the sword of the Spirit, which is the word of God; praying always with all prayer and supplication in the Spirit. (Ephesians 6:13–18)

The Belt of Truth

A phrase used quite often in the Bible is, "Gird up your loins." To understand this, we need to realize that in Bible days, both men and women wore long garments that extended below their knees. In order to do anything active, the first thing a person had to do was get those long garments up above the knees for free movement of the legs. In order to accomplish this, the person put a belt on, pulled the long garment up, and tucked it into the belt. After that, the person was ready for action. Unless someone did this, he couldn't go into action because the long garment would have impeded him.

How does this apply to us? I believe the "long garments" that encumber us can be religious language and behavior. We must be ruthlessly honest with ourselves and, as the Holy Spirit leads, with other people. We cannot encumber ourselves with religious clichés. They are a terrible hindrance if we want to be truly committed Christians. We cannot hide behind religious talk; we have to be sincere.

The Breastplate of Righteousness

The area of the body the breastplate protects is the heart. I have always been blessed by this statement of Solomon:

> *Watch over your heart with all diligence,*
> *for from it flow the springs of life.*
>   (Proverbs 4:23 NAS)

What we have in our heart will ultimately determine the course of our lives, for good or for evil. That is why it is essential that we protect our hearts from all kinds of evil and why Paul spoke about the breastplate of righteousness as a protection of the heart.

Paul returned to this theme of armor in another epistle and called it *"the breastplate of faith and love"* (1 Thessalonians 5:8 NAS). He described the breastplate from another point of view. If we put these two passages together, *"the breastplate of righteousness"* is a *"breastplate of faith and love."* This tells us the kind of righteousness Paul had in mind. Not the righteousness of works; not the righteousness of a religious law; but the righteousness that comes only by faith.

The Shoes of the Gospel

For this item of armor identified as shoes, I prefer to say "the boots of the preparation of the gospel of peace." Roman soldiers wore leather boots that were strapped all the way up the calf. These boots were firmly fixed on them. Scripture emphasizes that we must have our boots on. We have to be prepared to bring the message of the gospel of peace. The fact is, if we don't have peace in our own hearts, we really don't have much to transmit to others. We must believe and know the Scriptures. We must be able to point people to the truth of God's Word. This is the preparation of the gospel of peace.

The Shield of Faith

We see two kinds of shields spoken of in the New Testament: one is a small, round shield; the other is a long, oval shield that could cover the whole person. The shield spoken of here in this passage is the long, oval shield behind which a man could be totally covered. This is the shield of faith.

The Helmet of Salvation

What area of the person does the helmet protect? The mind. Because of my own struggles with depression, God showed me early on that I had to learn to protect my mind. When I asked

Him how, the answer came from the Word of God: the helmet of salvation.

When God made that truth clear to me, I said to myself, *I know I'm saved. Does that mean I already have the helmet of salvation?* The answer came when I saw that Paul was talking in this passage to people who were saved and baptized in the Spirit. Yet he still told them to take the helmet of salvation. We don't automatically have the helmet because we are saved. Clearly, we need to "put it on."

In 1 Thessalonians, we find a very useful cross-reference: *"And as a helmet, the hope of salvation"* (1 Thessalonians 5:8). It helped me greatly to discover that the nature of the helmet is hope. Just as faith protects our heart, hope protects our mind against depression and discouragement. Biblical faith is in the realm of the heart: *"With the heart one believes"* (Romans 10:10). But hope is in the realm of the mind. The writer of Hebrews said, *"Faith is the substance of things hoped for"* (Hebrews 11:1). So, on the basis of faith in the heart, we may have hope in the mind. And hope safeguards our minds.

The Sword of the Spirit

In the list of spiritual armor, there is one more

item of equipment: the sword of the Spirit—the Word of God. Many of us may already be familiar with the erudite distinctions between *logos* and *rhema*—*logos* being the eternal counsel of God and *rhema* being the Word of God spoken. This citation in Ephesians 6 tells us that the sword of the Spirit is the *rhema* of God. In other words, it is not the Bible on your bedside table; it is the Word of God operating when we speak it with our mouth. That is a sword. That is how Jesus used it when Satan confronted Him in the wilderness. Three times He said, *"It is written"* (Matthew 4:4–10, Luke 4:4–10). That is making the written word, logos, your *rhema*. And that's what drives Satan back.

The Seventh Weapon

When we analyze this list of six items of equipment, we see that, essentially, they are defensive weapons—all except the sword. It is an offensive weapon. Even then, we need to realize that the sword can only operate as far as our arm can reach. We cannot cast down Satan's kingdom without further weapons.

Whenever I find six of a good thing in the Bible (this is just my personal observation) I tend to look for the seventh. So as we examine the list of these six items, we need to look for the seventh. I believe the seventh weapon is presented at the end of the passage, *"Praying always with all prayer and supplication in the Spirit"* (Ephesians 6:18).

Prayer is our means of breaking out of the restrictions of reaching only as far as our arm will extend. Prayer is limitless. It is our "intercontinental ballistic missile." We can launch it from anywhere and make it land anywhere. In the weapon of prayer, there are three main components to do the job: the Word of God (the *logos*); the name of Jesus; and the blood of Jesus.

Although prayer is a powerful weapon, we need something to launch it. Any missile requires something to launch it. Any bomb requires something to drop it. Any bullet requires something to fire it. In the old days, any arrow required a bow to shoot it. I want to suggest that the same is true of the weapon of prayer. It requires some means of "launching" it. Remember that in regard to the seventh weapon against Satan's kingdom, we have the main components of the weapon: the Word of God, the name of Jesus, and the blood of Jesus. How do we get them to be operative against the kingdom of Satan? It is my experience that we have to make use of our four main ways to launch that seventh weapon: *prayer, praise, preaching,* and *testimony.*

But these four launching devices are only effective insofar as they are loaded with the Word of God, the name of Jesus, and the blood of Jesus (the primary components of the weapon of prayer).

Our Need for God's Power

Out of the mouth of babes and nursing infants You [God] *have ordained strength, because of Your enemies, that You may silence the enemy and the avenger.*

(Psalm 8:2)

Who is "the enemy and the avenger"? Satan. Who are the other enemies? Satan's kingdom, principalities, and powers in the heavenlies.

We must realize our need for God's supernatural power. Christianity is a religion of the supernatural. I once read through the book of Acts, examining it to see what would happen if I removed all reference to the manifestly supernatural. (Not just inward supernatural experiences, but actions that are visible—that can be perceived by the senses.) At the end of my study of the book of Acts, which has 28 chapters, I discovered that not one chapter out of the 28 would

be left intact if we eliminated the supernatural.
The only record we have in Scripture of how
the Church is intended to operate attests that we
cannot function effectively and accomplish the
will of God solely by our own natural ability. We
must have the supernatural enabling of the Holy
Spirit. And one main form of that enabling is the
list of supernatural gifts of the Holy Spirit in the
twelfth chapter of 1 Corinthians.

One statement by the apostle Paul summarizes
what I am saying: *"For the kingdom of God is not
in word, but in power"* (1 Corinthians 4:20).

It is not a matter of theology, although
theology certainly has its place. It is not a matter
of argument. It is not a matter of intellectual
proof. It is the demonstration of the supernatural
power of God.

I believe supernatural power is the primary
need of the Church today, especially when we
are surrounded by millions of Muslims. Nothing
will reach the Muslim mind more effectively than
the demonstration of the supernatural power of
God. And personally we have an unprecedented
opportunity. Instead of having to go to the
Muslims, they have come to us. In the past, we
could not go to their nations and proclaim the
gospel because we would have been put in prison
or executed. But God has arranged for Muslims
to come here. The question is: What is the Church

doing about it? It is time for the Church to rise up and declare, "We will demonstrate to them that Jesus is alive."

The Climax of Our Spiritual Battle

As we conclude our observations about our role in the war between the kingdom of God and the kingdom of Satan, let us look at the prophetic climax of this war from the book of Revelation:

> *And war broke out in heaven: Michael and his angels fought with the dragon; and the dragon and his angels fought, but they did not prevail, nor was a place found for them in heaven any longer. So the great dragon was cast out* [that old snake— that's the Prince version], *called the Devil and Satan who deceives the whole world.*
> (Revelation 12:7–9)

This passage gives us the most complete description of Satan in one verse. The word Devil (*diabolos* in Greek) means "a slanderer" or "a false accuser." *Satan* means "an enemy" or "an opposer." He is the slanderer who opposes God, the people of God, and the purposes of God, while deceiving the whole world.

The great dragon at this point is cast out of his kingdom in the heavenlies. This is not only the climax of the war, but also the description of us winning. That is why it is so important.

Then I heard a loud voice saying in heaven, "Now salvation, and strength, and the kingdom of our God, and the power [or authority] *of His Christ have come, for the accuser of our brethren, who accused them before our God day and night, has been cast down."* (v. 10)

In this passage, it is the angels who are talking. So when they say, *"our brethren,"* they are talking about us. So what is Satan doing right now? Accusing us. Where? Before the throne of God. That is a shocking fact, isn't it? And Satan is doing this accusing day and night. His sole purpose is to prove us guilty. (Just as a side note, we cannot truly defeat him until we know how to deal with his weapon of guilt.)

The Most Powerful Secret

I will now share what I consider to be the most powerful secret of Scripture that God has ever revealed to me. I regard this as extremely valuable:

And they overcame him by the blood of the Lamb and by the word of their testimony, and they did not love their lives to the death.   (Revelation 12:11)

Notice that this verse says, *"They overcame him."* Who is *they*? That refers to us. Who is *him*? Satan. Clearly, this is a direct conflict between the Church and Satan.

Remember that testimony was one of the four ways of launching the weapons. This means we overcome Satan when we testify personally to what the Word of God says the blood of Jesus does for us. Our testimony makes it personal. It takes the general truth of the Scripture and applies it personally to our lives.

In order to apply it effectively, we have to know what the Word of God says about the blood of Jesus. Otherwise we can't do it. Let us examine some of the statements of Scripture about the blood of Jesus.

Redemption

By the blood of Jesus, we are redeemed:

> *In Him* [Jesus] *we have redemption through His blood.* (Ephesians 1:7)

Redemption means we have been bought back. We were in the kingdom of Satan; we've been bought back out of the kingdom of Satan. The price of our redemption, Peter told us, was not silver or gold, but *"the precious blood of Christ, as of a lamb without blemish and without spot"* (1 Peter 1:19).

> *Let the redeemed of the LORD say so, whom He has redeemed from the hand of the enemy.* (Psalm 107:2)

We make this our personal testimony by saying out loud: "Through the blood of Jesus, I am redeemed out of the hand of the devil."

Cleansing

By the blood of Jesus, we are cleansed:

> *If we walk in the light as He is in the light, we have fellowship one with another, and the blood of Jesus Christ His Son cleanses us from all sin.* (1 John 1:7)

The words used in this passage are all in the continuing present tense: if we continually walk, we continually have fellowship, and the blood continually cleanses us. Bear in mind, it is conditional. If we are not walking in the light, the blood does not cleanse us. But by walking in the light, we have fellowship with fellow believers. If we are out of fellowship, we are out of the light. If we are out of the light, the blood doesn't cleanse us. That is an important truth to remember.

We make this personal by saying out loud: "While I am walking in the light, the blood of Jesus is cleansing me, now and continually, from all sin."

Justification

By the blood of Jesus, we are justified:

Having now been justified by His blood.
                                    (Romans 5:9)

Justified means, "acquitted, not guilty, made righteous, just-as-if-I'd never sinned."

We make this personal testimony by saying out loud: "Through the blood of Jesus, I am justified, acquitted, not guilty, made righteous, just-as-if-I'd never sinned."

Sanctification

By the blood of Jesus, we are sanctified:

Therefore Jesus also, that He might sanctify the people with His own blood, suffered outside the gate.

(Hebrews 13:12)

Sanctified has both a negative and a positive meaning. It means, negatively, "to be separated and set apart from sin." And, positively, it means, "to be made partaker of God's holiness."

We make this our personal testimony by saying out loud: "Through the blood of Jesus, I am sanctified, separated from sin and the kingdom of Satan, and made partaker of God's own holiness."

Now let us put these powerful testimonies all together and say them as a personal declaration:

"Through the blood of Jesus, I am redeemed out of the hand of the devil. While I'm walking in the light, the blood of Jesus is cleansing me, now and continually, from all sin. Through the blood of Jesus, I am justified, acquitted, not guilty, made righteous, just-as-if-I'd

*never sinned. Through the blood of Jesus,
I am sanctified, set apart from sin and
Satan's kingdom, and made partaker of
God's holiness."*

Once we have made this declaration, we have
great reason to begin to thank Him.

4

THE POWER OF THE CROSS

*For the message of the cross is foolishness
to those who are perishing, but to us who
are being saved it is the power of God.*

(1 Corinthians 1:18)

Over the last few chapters I have explained the absolute perfection of the redemptive work of Jesus on the cross. It covered every need that could ever arise in our lives. It was a perfect work. Through this work on the cross, Jesus administered a total, eternal, irrevocable defeat to Satan and his kingdom. This is the good news of the kingdom!

What could we suppose would be the devil's response to this work? What would he want to do about it? He would do his best to undermine the work of the cross. He would do his best to obscure the work of the cross, because once the work of the cross is obscured he could reassert his control over humanity. And that is precisely what the devil did, has done, and is doing. Clearly, one of his primary aims is to obscure what was accomplished by the death of Jesus on the cross.

Why Satan Obscures the Cross

We see three reasons for the devil's fierce efforts to obscure the power of the cross. First, it is the only basis of all God's provision for His redeemed people. There is no other basis.

> *For by one offering* [sacrifice] *God has perfected forever those who are being sanctified.*   *(Hebrews 10:14)*

By the sacrifice of Jesus on the cross, God has done all that will ever be needed for any human being in any period of history. It is all done through the cross.

Our appropriation of the work of the cross is progressive: we are *being* sanctified. What Jesus has done is perfect, finished, complete. But our appropriation is progressive. I don't believe any one person, myself included, has yet appropriated all that has been made available to us through the cross. As we go through the process of sanctification—being made holy, being conformed to God, thinking God's thoughts, living His way—we will appropriate more and more. But if the enemy moves in to obscure the power of the cross, although we should be living as children of the King, we will begin living like beggars and paupers. His goal is to obscure the fact that all the benefits God has provided come to us solely on the basis of the cross. Satan is very astute. He knows exactly what to strike at. He knows that if he can obscure the cross, he has the Church at his mercy.

The second reason the enemy wants to obscure the power of the cross is that it was the means of Satan's total defeat. In previous chapters we looked closely at God's redemptive work. Through the cross, Jesus ministered a total, eternal, irreversible defeat to Satan. Satan cannot change that. But what he can try to do is conceal that fact from us. The result would be that we no longer live in victory because we don't comprehend the victory that was won for us.

The third reason Satan obscures the power of the cross is that it is the only source of power for real Christian living. Some Christians and popular psychologists are fond of quoting the Sermon on the Mount as the way people ought to live. As good as that sermon was, the only way we get the ability to live in the manner it describes is through the sacrifice of Jesus on the cross. Jesus' sacrifice dealt with the old man, the fleshly nature. As Paul said, *"Our old man was crucified with Him"* (Romans 6:6), and a little later in Galatians he added, "Those who are Christ's have crucified the flesh with its passions and desires" (Galatians 5:24). Until we learn to apply the cross to our carnal nature, the nature will master us. We cannot master it.

Paul said in Romans 6:6, *"Our old man was crucified...that we should no longer be slaves of sin."* That is the provision of the cross. And once we grasp what Jesus accomplished on the cross in our lives, the devil is defeated.

Satan's "Fifth Column"

In 1936, there was a civil war in Spain between the left wing and the right wing. Tragically, the Spaniards were fighting against one another. At one point, a certain Spanish general was besieging a Spanish city. A second general came to him and said, "What is your plan to take this city?" The first general replied, "I have four columns advancing on the city, one from the north, one from the south, one from the east, and one from the west." Then he paused and said, "But it's my fifth column I'm expecting to take the city for me." The second general asked, "Where is your fifth column?" And he replied, "Inside the city." The fifth column is that which is inside, working against the people who are unaware of its presence.

That is Satan's tactic to destroy the Church. He has never been able to defeat the Church from without. But once he gets a fifth column inside, then he says, "It is my fifth column that will take the city."

In a sense, Satan's deceptive power, especially manifested in the form of witchcraft, is that fifth column inside the Church. This very theme is dealt with by Paul in Galatians, and in a real sense, it is the theme of the letter to the Galatians. We see this clearly in Paul's words at the beginning of the third chapter of Galatians:

O foolish Galatians! Who has bewitched you that you should not obey the truth, before whose eyes Jesus Christ was clearly portrayed among you as crucified?
(Galatians 3:1)

Let us focus on that rather strange question: "Who has bewitched you?" As we will see in the following verses, these Galatians had been saved, they had been baptized in the Holy Spirit, and they had seen God working miracles among them.

Nonetheless they were bewitched. What I am pointing out is this: the fact that we have been saved, baptized in the Spirit, and experienced miracles is no guarantee that we will not be bewitched by the deceptive power of the enemy—in a word, *witchcraft.*

But how did Paul know that witchcraft was operating? What was the evidence? The answer is very important and revealing. Witchcraft had obscured the revelation they had received of Jesus Christ crucified. In line with all we have seen in this chapter, the supreme aim of witchcraft in the Church was to hide the reality of Jesus Christ crucified.

The description of what happened in the following verses is also very revealing for us:

This only I want to learn from you: Did you receive the Spirit by the works of the law, or by the hearing of faith?

(Galatians 3:2)

Notice that the Galatians had received the Holy Spirit. Paul was asking them,

"How did you receive it; by keeping the Law of Moses or by hearing the gospel with faith?"

Are you so foolish? Having begun in the [Holy] Spirit, are you now being made perfect by the flesh? Have you suffered so many things in vain—if indeed it was in vain? Therefore He who supplies the Spirit to you and works miracles among you, does He do it by the works of the law, or by the hearing of faith? (vv. 3–5)

The root problem for the Galatians was that the reality of Jesus crucified had been obscured by an evil satanic power that had moved in. The two problems that resulted were carnality and legalism. They had gone back to fleshly attempts to do the will of God, to please God. They had reverted to keeping all sorts of rules as a way of achieving righteousness with God. By doing so, they had missed the purpose of Christ's death. Paul stated the final result this way:

For as many as are of the works of the law are under the curse; for it is written, "Cursed is everyone who does not continue in all things which are written in the book of the law, to do them." (Galatians 3:10)

Essentially, Paul was saying, "If you have gone back to trying to achieve righteousness by keeping the law, remember, you have got to keep the whole law all the time or you are under a curse." You see, when Israel came into the land of Canaan, one of the first things they had to do was to pronounce a curse upon themselves if they did not keep the whole law all the time. We must realize that keeping a little bit of the law some of the time does not do us any good. If we are going to be justified by keeping the law, we have to keep the whole law all the time. And none of us, in God's sight, can ever be justified by the works of the law. It is a deception of Satan, one that appeals primarily to human pride.

When I was in the British army years ago and came to know the Lord, I became a witness for the Lord. Because I lived a life that was very different from my fellow soldiers, many of them asked what had happened to me. They joked that I had "gotten religion." I would tell them, "No, I did not get religious. I got saved." Then I would tell them about salvation. Amazingly, the first reaction of almost everyone I talked with was to give me a little list of the rules they kept. Each one seemed to have a list tailored to his own particular life. In other words, the first reaction of man confronted with God's demand for righteousness is, "I'll keep a law." I have said the following words in many places, and sometimes I have shocked Christians with them: "Christianity is not a set of rules!" Once we reduce it to that, we have lost the vision of the cross. And if that happens, we have lost the power of God.

Lethal Legalism

Simply stated, the two marks of the work of witchcraft in the Galatian church were *legalism* and *carnality*. Wherever we encounter legalism, somewhere behind it is witchcraft. Legalism is the greatest single threat to the purposes of God. Some would say it is immorality and carnality. But, as a matter of fact, legalism actually promotes those two activities. How can that be so? If we are always telling people, "You must not lust," and that is all we give them, what happens? We are actually feeding lust. Paul said, *"I would not have known sin except through the law. For I would not have known covetousness unless the law had said, 'You shall not covet'"* (Romans 7:7). Negative rules operate in the area of the flesh, and they feed the very thing they are supposed to prevent.

Many people feel that if we don't make enough rules, we won't keep people under control. Well, they make fifteen rules and the people are not under control, so they make thirty rules and they're still not under control. So then they make sixty rules. But the more rules you create in order to make people good, the more you feed the carnal nature, and the carnal nature is incapable of producing anything good.

Galatians is very interesting among all of Paul's epistles. Galatians is the only epistle where Paul did not begin by thanking God for the people he was writing to. When he wrote to the Corinthian church, even though there was drunkenness at the Lord's Table, incest, and immorality, Paul still began by thanking God for the grace He had given to that church. But when Paul wrote to the Galatians, he was so worked up he did not give any thanks. Instead, he began by saying, *"I marvel that you are turning away so soon from Him who called you in the grace of Christ, to a different gospel"* (Galatians 1:6). What was the problem? Legalism. Paul viewed it as a much greater threat than immorality or drunkenness (not that we would ever suggest to condone those activities).

Let me now offer a definition of legalism. First of all, legalism is attempting to achieve righteousness with God by observing a set of rules. We know God has already ruled that out as a means of justification. He has said, "By the works of the law no flesh shall be justified in His sight" (Galatians 2:16). It is impossible.

Second, legalism is adding other requirements to what God has stated for achieving righteousness with Him. The requirements for achieving righteousness with God are very simply stated in Romans: if you believe in Him who delivered Jesus our Lord to death for our offenses, and raised Him again from the dead for our justification, you are righteous. (See Romans 4:22–25.)

There is no other way to achieve righteousness with God. Nothing else can be added. No person, no Church, no group, no preacher has the authority to add any other requirement to achieving righteousness with God than those which are stated in the New Testament. Legalism is either attempting to achieve righteousness with God by observing a set of rules, or it is adding to the requirements that God has stated in the New Testament.

5

THE NATURE OF WITCHCRAFT

For rebellion is as the sin of witchcraft,
and stubbornness is as iniquity and
idolatry.
(1 Samuel 15:23)

In these words spoken by the prophet Samuel to King Saul, Samuel made two comparisons addressing two very sinful attitudes: rebellion and stubbornness. The statement reveals God's evaluation of them both. Rebellion is a twin of witchcraft; stubbornness is a twin of idolatry.

First, let us consider stubbornness. The verse says stubbornness is a form of idolatry. How does that occur? The stubborn person makes idols out of his own opinions. In that light, it is very interesting to consider our attitude in the Church today. Generally, we will not accept drunkards or openly immoral people. But how many stubborn people do we have in Church? In God's eyes, they are idolaters. In most churches, if somebody came in with a wooden idol, fell down and worshiped it in front of everyone, we would not tolerate that. But, alas, we tolerate a lot of stubborn people, and often we let them get away with it. In God's sight, they are idolaters.

Let us now focus more intently on rebellion. The verse indicates that the root of witchcraft is rebellion. Wherever you find rebellion you can anticipate witchcraft. I learned this in the ministry of deliverance. For instance, I learned that if a person needed deliverance from a spirit of witchcraft, almost invariably they also needed deliverance from rebellion. And conversely, where I would encounter a spirit of rebellion, I would check to see if there was not also a spirit of witchcraft. They are closely related.

Rebellion rejects God's legitimate authority, just as king Saul rejected the authority of God's Word. We cannot exist in life for long without authority. So if we don't have legitimate authority, illegitimate authority will replace the void. Where we have illegitimate authority, it has to be supported by wrongful power. The illegitimate power that supports rebellion is the power of witchcraft. So really, wherever we find illegitimate authority being exercised, we need to be prepared to deal with witchcraft.

We see a very clear example of this in the United States in the 1960s. Young people turned their backs on almost all accepted forms of authority— parents, church, government, whatever—and they became a generation of rebels. Over the years, I have dealt with many of those "rebels," and many of them who met the Lord are my friends today. But almost without exception, all who went into rebellion also went into the occult, the satanic supernatural, and witchcraft. This is the logic of spiritual experience. It is almost impossible to be deeply involved in rebellion without sooner or later coming under the power of witchcraft.

If we go back to the example of king Saul for a moment, we remember in his story that he disobeyed Samuel's injunction to slaughter all the animals that had been captured. Instead, he kept "the best"—as he called it—to offer to God. God said, "I am not interested in your sacrifice, because it comes out of disobedience." As king of Israel, Saul had actually put out all the witches from Israel. (See 1 Samuel 28:3.) But just before his death—when he could not hear from God—he himself sought a witch (v. 7) out of desperation. That is not an accident; it is cause and effect. I want to emphasize this point: wherever there is rebellion, sooner or later there will be witchcraft.

Let me emphasize one other point: when you deal with witchcraft (the satanic supernatural, the occult in all its forms), if you only deal with the occult, you have not dealt with the root, because the root is rebellion.

Two Aspects of Witchcraft

Witchcraft has two aspects, a natural aspect and a supernatural aspect. Many people do not realize that witchcraft is listed as a work of the flesh. It is an expansion of the fallen human nature.

Now the works of the flesh are evident, which are: adultery, fornication, uncleanness, lewdness, idolatry, sorcery.
                                   (Galatians 5:19)

The King James Version uses the term *witchcraft* instead of *sorcery*. Regardless of which version you use, you have the same meaning: witchcraft is a work of the flesh. That means it is an expression of the unregenerate nature of fallen man. It is what naturally comes out of our fleshly nature. In our fallen nature, we desire to control people. We desire to get people to do what we want, and very often we use illegitimate means to make that happen.

Three Expressions of Witchcraft in the Flesh

This operation of witchcraft has three key words, and when these three activities are happening, whether you realize it or not, it is an encounter with witchcraft. The three key words are: *dominate*, *manipulate*, and *intimidate*. The end purpose is *control*—or the need to dominate. To achieve this domination, depending on the situation, a person will either use manipulation or intimidation to do it.

Remember, this is in the natural; we're not talking about anything supernatural yet. Witchcraft, as a work of the flesh, operates in every area of society. Let me give you a few examples. Whether people like it or not, God has ordained a certain structure in the family. The husband is identified as the head of the wife. (See Ephesians 5:23.) Regardless of people's attempts to stand the family on its head, God hasn't changed the order. Beneath the authority of husband and wife are the children who, in God's order, are subject to the authority of their parents.

Witchcraft will operate in that context through

either manipulation or intimidation to set aside the divinely authorized order.

Let's take children first. Children can be manipulators at any age. A child of five learns to use manipulation. Suppose a mother is hosting guests and serving cookies. The small child knows that her mother does not want her to have cookies. But she knows that when guests are there, it is very difficult for Mother to say no. So while the guests are there, she comes in and says, "Mama, may I have a cookie?" You can guess what the mother will do. She will probably give in. When that happens, she has been manipulated.

Witchcraft can be found in mothers and fathers too. The most common way for witchcraft to operate in a woman is manipulation. In a man, it is intimidation. But each of them has the same aim: to control the other. So, if the wife does not get her way, she throws a tearful fit, withholds affection, and makes her husband's life miserable. In the end, what does he do? He gives in. With the husband it can happen just as frequently, but the husband may be a brute, a strong man with a bad temper. If he does not get his way, he shouts and becomes violent and threatens, and the whole family tiptoes around him. The one thing they want to avoid is another fit of temper by Daddy. What is he doing? He is intimidating them. His aim is to get his own way.

It can well be that a husband and wife will have differences. The divine order is that they talk it out face-to-face, and prayerfully seek God. But manipulation never faces the real issues. It always goes behind. The real issues are never brought out into the light. Millions of married couples never really bring their differences out into the open. But each tries to go behind the other to get what he or she wants. That is manipulation.

Biblical Examples of Witchcraft

Two examples from the Bible of witchcraft on a higher level are Delilah and Jezebel. In the case of Delilah, although Samson was the strong man of the Bible, Delilah was stronger yet. Scripture tells us Delilah pressed upon Samson; she wore him out; she cried; she had moods. She said to him, "You don't really love me. You haven't told me your secret." Ultimately, Delilah wore him down. (See Judges 16:4–22.) I believe there are few men strong enough to deal with witchcraft in a woman. Very few. I have seen strong men who might be the president and CEO of an organization. But when it comes to dealing with a wife, they are manipulated.

The other example from Scripture is Jezebel. She was by no means a sweet woman. But she knew how to get her husband Ahab to do what she wanted. In reality, she took over ruling Israel, reinforcing the principles we discussed earlier: usurpation and illegitimate authority. It is interesting that Jezebel is referred to in the New Testament in Revelation 2 as being inside the Church. The New Testament warns us that witchcraft is going to infiltrate the Church, and in many instances, we can see it already.

There are many examples of manipulation in the Church. We will take a typical Pentecostal congregation, for example. A young pastor, in his first pastorate has about a hundred people in the congregation. He is a little bit nervous and timid. In his congregation, there are two very spiritual sisters. Not just spiritual, but super-spiritual, and they know how the church ought to be run. Rather than sitting down prayerfully and talking it over with the pastor, one of them gets a tongue and the other comes up with the interpretation. Between them, they end up telling the pastor what to do through this method. What is that? Manipulation.

So we see that witchcraft as a work of the flesh has three trademarks: manipulation, intimidation, and domination. Wherever you encounter these activities, behind them is the power of witchcraft. When your eyes are opened to this reality, it is much easier to deal with it. These are real and relevant issues I am talking about. They are not occurring in some other country or on some other planet. They are happening all around us in the Church, our homes, and in our families. Witchcraft never came to do any of us any good. Remember what Jesus said, "The thief does not come except to steal, and to kill, and to destroy" (John 10:10). If you entertain the thief, you can expect him to do exactly those three things.

Witchcraft's Supernatural Aspect

We have seen that witchcraft is a work of the flesh. Now let's explore the fact that witchcraft is not merely a work of the flesh, but an evil, spiritual power. I believe that was the power that had moved into the Galatian church. What we are talking about is something supernatural. It is more than just human ability. We must recognize that not all supernatural manifestations come from God. A lot of them come from Satan. There are, I believe, only two sources of the supernatural available to men: God or Satan. Any supernatural power that does not come from God does, in fact, come from Satan. God's kingdom is a kingdom of light. In God's kingdom, we are aware of whose we are and what God is doing because it occurs "in the light."

But Satan's kingdom is a kingdom of darkness. In that kingdom, we are not aware of what is manipulating us, what is controlling us, what is driving us, because it occurs "in the darkness."

There are three main branches of the supernatural aspect of witchcraft as described in the English language. They are *witchcraft*, *divination*, and *sorcery*. They cover the whole field of the satanic supernatural, and I will describe each one and provide a scriptural example of each one.

Witchcraft

Witchcraft is the power branch. Its product is power, and it operates through such activities as spells and curses. Perhaps the single most powerful weapon of witchcraft is curses, which is a very old practice. In Numbers 22, we find the story of Balaam, who was what we might call a witch doctor. In verse 10, Balaam is actually explaining to God the proposition he got from Balak:

> *Balak the son of Zippor, king of Moab, has sent to me, saying, "Look, a people has come out of Egypt, and they cover the face of the earth* [speaking of Israel]. *Come*

now, curse them for me; perhaps I shall
be able to overpower them and drive them
out."   (Numbers 22:10–11)

This was standard practice in the cultures of the Bible. It was normal for kings or others going to war not merely to fight on the natural plane, but to make war on the supernatural plane as well. They would get their witch doctor to curse their enemy. (There exists a list of curses pronounced by the Egyptian pharaohs in the 19th century B.C. against 66 different nations.) It was an attempt to bring them to a place where they could be defeated in war. When Goliath came against David, he cursed him in the name of his gods. That was not just a display of vulgarity. He was really asserting: "My gods can deal with your God."

In a certain sense, ancient warfare was not just a conflict between nations. It was viewed as a test of power between the gods of those nations. For instance, when God dealt with Egypt and brought Israel out, the psalm says that He judged the gods of Egypt—not just the natural rulers, but also the spiritual rulers. (See Exodus 12:12, Jeremiah 43:12, Psalm 135:8–10, 82:1.) Balaam was hired because he was a good curser; that was his profession.

Divination

The second branch we will examine is divination, which in most modern translations is called "fortune-telling." Divination is the knowledge branch of witchcraft. The product is not power, but knowledge, which, as I pointed out, first led man into sin. The scriptural example in Acts 16 is very clear, describing what happened when Paul and Silas first arrived to preach the gospel in Philippi:

> *Now it happened as we went to prayer, that a certain slave girl possessed with a spirit of divination met us.* (Acts 16:16)

The Greek actually says, "having a spirit of python" or "a python spirit," in other words, a snake spirit. Remember, snakes have always been regarded in pagan society as the source of unusual knowledge and wisdom. It is significant to note that what this girl said was absolutely true. She did not know it by natural means; she knew it by supernatural means. She was just a simple slave girl who had this ability. But she *"brought her masters much profit by fortune-telling"* (v. 16). (Because she was a slave, the profit did not go to her. It went to her masters.)

This girl followed Paul and us, and cried out, saying, "These men are the servants of the Most High God, who proclaim to us the way of salvation." (v. 17)

The amazing fact is that what she said was absolutely true. In the past, I have commented that in contemporary missions such a young lady might have been made a charter member of the Church forever. She was the first person to recognize who Paul and Silas really were. But Paul knew that she did it not by God's Spirit, but by a divining spirit, a fortune-telling spirit. In the end, he turned around and commanded it to come out in the name of Jesus. When it came out, she was no longer able to tell fortunes. Her masters were so angry at the profits they would lose that they brought Paul and Silas before the magistrates, and the rest, as they say, is history. (Read the remainder of Acts 16.) The whole city was in an uproar because a single slave girl was delivered of a spirit of divination.

At that point, Paul was not merely dealing with Satan's kingdom on the natural, physical plane, but consequently Satan's kingdom in the heavenlies intervened because their strategy against the Church was being frustrated. It is remarkable to note that almost everywhere Paul went there was a riot. Later, in 2 Corinthians, he said that there was an angel of Satan to buffet him. (See 2 Corinthians 12:7.) I believe that was not a metaphor. It was just as he said. He battled a satanic angel that organized a riot in every city where Paul went. Why don't we have riots? Maybe we don't bother Satan enough! I believe when the Church is what it ought to be, there will be a lot more riots. There will also be a lot more revivals. I don't know how many revivals we can have without riots. We have to decide, "Is it worth the price?"

Sorcery

The third branch we will examine is the sorcery branch. Frequently, but not exclusively, sorcery operates through objects such as potions or charms. Basically this would include anything that is called lucky, such as a horseshoe, a rabbit's foot, and all things that people carry to bring them luck. Sorcery also operates through love potions, which is fairly common. A woman would say, "I want this man to fall in love with me, so I'll go to the witch doctor and get a potion, and put it in his food. After that he'll fall in love with me."

My wife Ruth and I were in Zambia together with some Christian brothers and sisters. During our time there, we offered a prayer for all the women who were barren and could not have children. For Africans, that is a real disaster. About four hundred professing Christian ladies presented themselves for prayer. Before we prayed, however, someone asked the question, "How many of you went to the witch doctor for a potion to deliver you from barrenness?" All but two of them raised their hands! It made us realize we are not dealing with practices that are rare or uncommon.

Sorcery also operates through drugs. The Greek word for sorcery is directly formed from the Greek word for "a drug." The entire drug culture is a clear example of sorcery at work. Almost all of those people, as they come to Jesus, will need to be delivered from that power.

Let us look at just one picture of sorcery in Revelation 9. This passage describes a future scene in human history when God's judgments are being manifested and are falling on the wicked:

> *But the rest of mankind, who were not killed by these plagues, did not repent of the works of their hands, that they should not worship demons, and idols of gold, silver, brass, stone, and wood, which can neither see nor hear nor walk and they did not repent of their murders or their*

> *sorceries or their sexual immorality or*
> *their thefts.*   (Revelation 9:20–21)

Together with sorcery goes sexual immorality and violence. I believe the tremendous upsurge of violence in our contemporary civilization is largely the work of sorcery. When we pray about these issues, beyond praying about the branch, we need to deal with the root—sorcery.

Witchcraft Produces Illegitimate Authority

We have already seen that witchcraft, expressed as rebellion, produces and supports an illegitimate authority. Rebellion has manifested itself through specific activities in the Church that are produced illegally. I will cite examples, including the alternatives that are subverted in this process.

The Carnal over the Spiritual

Witchcraft promotes the carnal and suppresses the spiritual. In terms of Old Testament patterns, witchcraft puts Ishmael over Isaac. That is precisely what Islam has done. Islam teaches that

Abraham did not sacrifice Isaac, but Ishmael. Muslims believe that Ishmael is the appointed heir. That is witchcraft putting Ishmael over Isaac. Of course, there are a lot more "Ishmaels" than this one example from Islam. Anything we do of our own initiative, which is not initiated by God through the Holy Spirit, will be an Ishmael. Jesus never did anything by His own initiative. He said, *"The Son can do nothing of Himself, but what He sees the Father do"* (John 5:19). The moment we try to start something that isn't initiated by God, we are going to produce an Ishmael. Abraham's experience should be a stern warning to us. Four thousand years ago Abraham produced Ishmael, and for all the ensuing years, the appointed seed of Abraham has had problems with Ishmael. These problems are coming to a climax in the Middle East right now.

Theology over Revelation

Witchcraft produces theology and sets it over revelation. This is one of the major problems of the Church. I would have to say, frankly, that many seminaries today are putting out servants of Satan. That is a shocking, but true, statement. Most of the problems of the Church result from exalting human thinking above divine revelation. This is certainly not true of all seminaries, but in my opinion, it is true of the many seminaries today.

Education over Discipling

Witchcraft in the Church exalts education above discipling. If we were to go to a theological seminary or a Bible school and sit for three years in classes, we would get a lot of head knowledge. What does knowledge do? It puffs up. Jesus didn't do that. He made His disciples follow behind Him and serve Him. If we don't combine training with serving, we are going to produce the wrong results. The only safeguard against giving people knowledge is enabling them to serve.

Psychology over Discernment

Witchcraft exalts psychology above discernment. In other words, psychological treatment over a legitimate word of knowledge. When Jesus met the woman at the well, He didn't ask her about her childhood, when she was born, whether she had problems with her parents, or whether there was a social stigma in her life. He just said, "You've had five husbands." And that was all He needed to say. One word of knowledge eliminates a whole lot of psychology.

Programs over Supernatural Direction

Witchcraft exalts programs above supernatural direction. The apostles never came up with a program for evangelizing Judea. They were simply sent out by the Holy Spirit. There was no program for sending Philip to Samaria. He just ended up there. And the results followed.

Eloquence over Supernatural Power

Witchcraft exalts eloquence above supernatural power. Jesus never gave His disciples training in homiletics. Charles Finney once said, "All the homiletical training that I've ever seen has had one aim—to make people speak as if they really meant what they were saying." Paul was a very highly educated man, and yet he said:

> *And I, brethren, when I came to you, did not come with excellence of speech or of wisdom declaring to you the testimony of God. For I determined not to know anything among you, except Jesus Christ and Him crucified.* (1 Corinthians 2:1–2)

In effect, he was saying, "I am not going to let witchcraft obscure Jesus and the cross." This is significant because Paul had just been to Athens before he went to Corinth. In Athens he had tried to meet the people on their own ground. He quoted Greek poets, and he met them on an intellectual basis, but the results were very disappointing. I suppose somewhere between Athens and Corinth, Paul said, "That's the end of that! From now on, all I'm going to do is present Jesus crucified." And the results in Corinth were tremendous: one of the largest churches in the early world took root and grew there.

But Paul had to make a decision: *"I determined not to know anything ... except Jesus Christ and Him crucified"* (1 Corinthians 2:2). Without question, witchcraft opposes the revelation of Jesus crucified.

> *I was with you in weakness, in fear, and in much trembling. And my speech and my preaching were not with persuasive words of human wisdom, but in demonstration of the Spirit and of power.* (vv. 3–4)

Those are the alternatives: human eloquence or supernatural demonstration.

Reasoning over Faith

Witchcraft exalts reasoning above the walk of faith. God doesn't lead us by reasoning; He leads us step-by-step in a walk of faith. As He dealt with Abraham, He deals with us. He doesn't tell us the whole plan of where we're going to go, or what's going to happen. He simply says, "This is the next move." As we walk in faith, we have the supernatural attestation of the Holy Spirit with us. When we rely on our own reasoning, all we receive is what reason can produce.

Legalism over Love

Finally, witchcraft exalts legalism above love. Doesn't it seem true that most legalistic, religious people are very unloving? Basically, we shy away from them. We don't want them wagging their finger at us and telling us, "Don't do this," and "Don't do that." They are very critical of others. Anybody that doesn't keep their set of rules is wrong.

> *For in Christ Jesus neither circumcision nor uncircumcision avails anything, but faith working through love.*
>
> (Galatians 5:6)

What really matters most is faith working through love. And notice what kind of faith. It is not a theological faith, nor a faith that majors on doctrinal hairsplitting. It is a faith that operates through love.

Each of the above tactics is part of Satan's diabolical strategy to obscure Jesus crucified. Once the Church loses sight of what was accomplished on the cross, the Church can no longer administer Jesus' victory over Satan. Witchcraft has blinded the eyes of the Church to miss this essential, fundamental truth. We must make a determined effort to throw off the veil of witchcraft and fix our gaze on the work of the cross.

6

THE WORK OF THE CROSS

For the message of the cross is
foolishness to those who are perishing,
but to us who are being saved it is the
power of God.

(1 Corinthians 1:18)

Let us keep in the forefront of our minds, as we have seen throughout this book, that on the cross Jesus administered to Satan a total, eternal, irrevocable defeat. Nothing can ever change that. Satan can never recover from that defeat, but Jesus has left it to the Church to administer His victory. So Satan's tactic is to keep the Church from advancing by obscuring what happened on the cross. As I stated in the previous chapter, the evil force that obscures the work of the cross is called witchcraft.

The Church today is similar to the condition of the Galatian Church as described by Paul:

*O foolish Galatians! Who has bewitched
you that you should not obey the truth,
before whose eyes Jesus Christ was clearly
portrayed among you as crucified?*

(Galatians 3:1)

What has witchcraft done? It has obscured
Jesus crucified. Once the Church loses sight of
what was accomplished on the cross, it can no
longer administer Jesus' victory over Satan.

We must be careful to safeguard ourselves,
and the safeguards all come through applying the
work of the cross in our own lives. There are two
aspects to the work of the cross: what Jesus did for
us, and what He will do in us. First, He provided
everything we will ever need and He defeated our
enemy. That is what Jesus did for us. However,
many people who get excited about what He did
for us have never begun to understand what the
cross is intended to do *in* us. If the cross does not
have its work in us, we will not fully benefit from
the victory because our subtle, deceptive enemy
will get the better of us and corrupt us.

Let us now focus on the five operations of the
cross in the life of the believer. In a sense, this
is not popular preaching. I am not going to tell
you how to get rich quick, how to solve all your
problems, or how to get all your prayers answered
in the next six months. I am going to outline for

you the vital truth of the victorious work of the cross. Let me preface it by saying emphatically that Jesus was never more victorious than when He was on the cross.

1. DELIVERANCE FROM THIS PRESENT EVIL AGE

Grace to you and peace from God the Father and our Lord Jesus Christ, who gave Himself for our sins, that He might deliver us from this present evil age, according to the will of our God and Father.   (Galatians 1:3–4)

The Present World Order

This first point is, I believe, the primary deliverance. Until we understand that it is God's purpose, through the cross, that we be delivered from this present evil age, we are not really aligned with what God intends to do for us and through us. Four other deliverances through the cross follow in Galatians, and we will look at each of them. But I believe the other four are the outworking of this primary deliverance, which is from this present evil age. Do we fully realize that it is God's purpose to deliver us from this present evil age?

Two Greek words in the New Testament describing our current society are not always accurately translated, so we need to examine them. The first word, *kosmos*— from which we get such words as *cosmonaut* and *cosmology*—is properly translated "world." But it doesn't refer to "the globe" as it is used in the New Testament. It means, "the present world order." The distinctive feature of the present world order is that it is not submitted to the righteous government of God. It is an order in rebellion against God. The Church, on the other hand, is a group of people called out from the world. That is what the word Church means: "a called out company." In John chapter 15, the word *world* occurs five times in one verse. This is what Jesus said to His disciples:

> *If you were of the world, the world would love its own. Yet because you are not of the world, but I chose you out of the world, therefore the world hates you.*

> (John 15:19)

We see here a total line of separation between the world and the Church. The world is in rebellion against God. The Church, called out by a sovereign choice of Jesus to become the people of God, is submitted to God. The more the Church is submitted to God, the more the world will hate it.

Jesus said to His brothers, *"The world cannot hate you* [because you belong to it]; *but it hates Me, because I testify of it that its deeds are evil"* (John 7:7 NAS). If the world doesn't hate the Church today, it is because the world is halfway inside the Church. Why should the world hate its own? There is a modern day teaching that the Church is going to take over the world. I don't believe that. At the present moment, it is the other way around. The world has taken over the Church. If the world was evicted from the Church and the Church was separated from the world, we would discover how much the world really hates the Church.

The Present Evil Age

The second Greek word used in the New Testament for modern society is the word *aion*, which gives us the English word "eon", meaning "an age." It's a measurement of time. God's time plan consists of ages that follow one another, and the strongest phrase in the Bible, "forever and ever," means "to the ages of ages."[1] The meaning is "ages, each of which is made up of ages." The human mind can't even begin to comprehend the depth of that phrase.

Here is the way the word age appears in Galatians: "[Christ] *gave Himself for our sins, that He might deliver us from this present evil age*" (Galatians 1:4).

Certain simple, objective facts are revealed in the Bible about this present age. First of all, the most important fact is that it is coming to an end. It is not going to last forever. All of us might say, "Thank God!" for that. Personally, I don't want the present age to continue. I think it is a mess, and it is getting steadily worse.

"Age" also appears in Matthew 13. In this great parable of the kingdom, Jesus is interpreting the significance of the wheat and the tares.

> *The enemy who sowed* [the tares] *is the devil, the harvest is the end of the age, and the reapers are the angels.*
>
> (Matthew 13:39)

Jesus said the harvest is the end of the age. The following verses reveal that when the harvest comes, the age is going to end.

> *Therefore as the tares are gathered and*

*burned in the fire, so it will be at the end
of this age. The Son of Man will send out
His angels, and they will gather out of His
kingdom all things that offend, and those
who practice lawlessness, and will cast
them into the furnace of fire. There will be
wailing and gnashing of teeth. Then the
righteous will shine forth as the sun in the
kingdom of their Father. He who has ears
to hear, let him hear!*

(Matthew 13:40–43)

The righteous and the wicked are going to
coexist right up to the end of the age. We need to
keep in mind that it is not our business to separate
them. It is too difficult. The workers said, "Shall
we go and pull up the tares?" (vv. 28–29) and the
landowner said, "No, because you might pull up
some of the wheat with them." But Jesus said,
"At the end of the age, I'll send out My angels.
They'll pull out the tares and the wheat will be
left." In the same chapter, in the parable of the
dragnet, Jesus said:

*So it will be at the end of the age. The
angels will come forth, separate the
wicked from among the just, and cast them
into the furnace of fire.*   (vv. 49–50)

It is extremely important for us to realize that this age is coming to an end. If we live as if it were to go on forever, we will be living in a delusion.

The next fact about this age states the reason why it is an evil age.

> *But even if our gospel is veiled, it is veiled to those who are perishing, whose minds the god of this age has blinded.*
>
> (2 Corinthians 4:3–4)

The God of This Age

Who blinds the minds of unbelievers? Satan. And what is he? He is "the god of this age." No wonder he doesn't want the age to end. Because when this age ends, he will no longer be a god. But the Church's responsibility is to bring the age to an end, thereby terminating the rule of Satan as a god.

In the sixth chapter of Hebrews, the writer spoke of those people who had deep spiritual experiences tasting the powers of a new age. But those same people had later gone back from what they had experienced.

> *For it is impossible for those who were*

once enlightened, and have tasted the
heavenly gift, and have become partakers
of the Holy Spirit, and have tasted the
good word of God and the powers of the
age to come.   (Hebrews 6:4–5)

There are five experiences there: We have
been enlightened, we have tasted the heavenly
gift (eternal life), we have become partakers of
the Holy Spirit, we have tasted the good Word
of God, and we have savored the powers of the
age to come. To me, that is what comes with
the baptism in the Holy Spirit. When you are
baptized in the Holy Spirit, you are immersed in
a supernatural presence. It is supernatural in this
age and will be natural in the next age. In this, we
have been given a little taste of what the power
of the next age will be like. God has given us a
taste in order to spoil our taste for this age. Why
should Christians be enamored with the tastes of
this age when we have tasted the powers of the
age to come?

Resisting This Age

Now he who received seed among the
thorns is he who hears the word, and the
cares of this world and the deceitfulness

> *of riches choke the word, and he becomes*
> *unfruitful.*   (Matthew 13:22)

Where it says *world* in this translation, the correct translation is "age" (as in the NIV). The worries of this age choke the Word of God and make us unfruitful. We cannot afford to be part of "this age," because, if we are, we will be dominated by its cares and its problems. They will make us spiritually unfruitful. We have to live lives that belong to a different age.

> *And do not be conformed to this world* [the correct translation is: "do not be conformed to this age"], *but be transformed by the renewing of your mind, that you may prove what is that good and acceptable and perfect will of God.* (Romans 12:2)

We cannot afford to be conformed to the present age. Our solution is not a list of religious rules, because that doesn't change people on the inside. The solution is for our minds to be changed, because when we begin to think differently, we will live differently. That is the difference between religion and grace. Religion consists of outside rules—what we should wear, how short our hair must be, how much lipstick we may wear, and other external observances. Paul essentially said, "Don't think the way this age thinks. Be changed in your mind. Let the Holy Spirit give you a different way of thinking and evaluating things, different priorities, different ambitions, different goals. Then you'll live differently."

Then Paul explained that when our mind is renewed, we will discover the good, acceptable, and perfect will of God. Many Christians don't find the will of God because they are never renewed in their minds. The unrenewed mind cannot discover the will of God. The carnal mind is enmity against God. God doesn't reveal His secrets to His enemies. But if our minds are changed, then God will begin to show us His secrets, including His plan for our lives. Millions of Christians will get to heaven, but I'm afraid they will have missed God's plan here on earth because they were not renewed in their minds. That is why we are not to be conformed to this present age.

The second book of Timothy tells of one of the great tragedies of the New Testament. One of Paul's most trusted, long-term fellow workers abandoned him. *"Demas has forsaken me, having loved this present world* [age]" (2 Timothy 4:10).

It doesn't say that Demas went into sin, that he

became immoral or drunk. He just was enamored of this present age. He reached a point where the love of this age made it impossible for him to go any further with Paul. I think that has been true in the experience of many people called to serve the Lord. The love of this age has kept them from fulfilling their call. A servant of God cannot love this present age. We have to make up our minds to resist the present age.

Results of Deliverance from This Present Age

There are two distinct results of being delivered from this present evil age.

Citizenship in Heaven

> *Brethren, join in following my example, and note those who so walk, as you have us for a pattern. For many walk, of whom I have told you often, and now tell you even weeping, that they are the enemies of the cross of Christ.* (Philippians 3:17–18)

Notice, they are not the enemies of Christ, but of the cross. In other words, as long as they can get what they want from Him, they will be friends.

> *Whose end is destruction, whose god is their belly, and whose glory is in their shame; who set their mind on earthly things.*   (v. 19)

Paul outlined the result of refusing to embrace the cross. We can say nice things about Jesus Christ and call Him our Savior, but if we don't embrace His cross, this will be our destination. For many modern Christians, their god is their belly. To tell the truth, they are more interested in what they put in their stomachs than what they can do for God. No race, ethnicity, or nationality is exempt from that problem.

Yet for those who resist this temptation, Paul said, *"For our citizenship is in heaven"* (Philippians 3:20).

Citizenship in heaven; what does that mean for us? I have British citizenship and American citizenship. I'm privileged. But the most important citizenship I have is citizenship in heaven. That's the only one that really matters. That's the result of embracing the cross and being separated from this present evil age. If you are a Christian, then your citizenship is in heaven. If you have citizenship in any nation, you're entitled to the passport of that nation. When you come to the nation where you're a citizen, you are admitted on very different terms than people who don't have that passport. Have you ever stood in the line and watched? My wife is only an American citizen, so when I come to Britain with her, I come in with my American passport. We stand in the line that says, "Other Passports." Everyone with a UK passport just walks right through. But when we get to the United States, then it's the other people who have to wait and we walk right through. It's important to have the right passport. And you can only have the right passport if you have the right citizenship. You need citizenship in heaven to have heaven's passport—the right of free entry into the country of which you're a citizen.

Looking for Christ's Return

Not only do we have citizenship in heaven. We are also looking for Christ's return. That is the second mark of being delivered from this present evil age. Paul expressed it this way:

> *For our citizenship is in heaven, from which we also eagerly wait for the Savior, the Lord Jesus Christ.* (Philippians 3:20)

Are we eagerly waiting for the Lord Jesus Christ? He is only coming back for the people who are eagerly waiting for Him.

> *And as it is appointed for men to die once, but after this the judgment, so Christ was offered once to bear the sins of many. To those who eagerly wait for Him He will appear a second time, apart from sin, for salvation.*   (Hebrews 9:27–28)

He will appear to those who eagerly wait for Him. If we have not been delivered from this present evil age, we will not be eagerly waiting for Jesus. So, the practical results of being delivered from this present evil age through faith in Jesus are that we have citizenship in heaven and we are eagerly awaiting the return of the Lord from heaven.

2. DELIVERANCE FROM THE LAW

We turn now to Galatians and the second deliverance provided by the cross. As I said earlier, these remaining four deliverances are different aspects of the primary deliverance: "from this present evil age." This means that to be delivered from this present evil age fully, we need to make sure that we have all four subsequent deliverances as well.

> *For I through the law died to the law that I might live to God.*   (Galatians 2:19)

When Christ died, I died to the law. My old man was crucified with Him. So, through the cross and the death of Jesus—which has become my death through my faith—I have died to the law. That's a wonderful thought, if we can grasp it. The last thing the law can do to us is put us to death. That is its final penalty. When it has put us to death, it can do nothing more to us. If a person is executed, he is no longer subject to the law. The only way out from the law is death. In the mercy of God, our death took place when Jesus died on the cross. "I through the law am dead to the law" (Galatians 2:19 KJV). The law has nothing to say to me; I have no more relationship to the law. I've been separated from the law by the death of Jesus.

When I would speak on this theme, I often saw a look of polite astonishment come on people's faces. They simply could not conceive that God's purpose is that we should be delivered from the law. But that is the truth. It is His purpose. It is clearly stated in the Bible many times. Here is one breathtaking statement:

For sin shall not have dominion over you, for you are not under law but under grace.   (Romans 6:14)

Previously in this book, I referred to two mutually exclusive alternatives: the law and grace. We can't have them both; we have to make a choice. If we are under law, we are not under grace. If we are under grace, we are not under law. So we have to make up our minds: am I under law or am I under grace? We can't have one foot in two different worlds.

The implication of this truth is that if we are under the law, sin will have dominion over us. What is the obvious conclusion? The only way to escape the dominion of sin is to escape from the law. This option was provided by the death of Jesus on the cross. "I through the law am dead to the law."

For when we were in the flesh, the sinful passions which were aroused by the law were at work in our members to bear fruit to death. But now we have been delivered from the law, having died to what we

were held by, so that we should serve in
the newness of the Spirit and not in the
oldness of the letter.   (Romans 7:5–6)

Paul was not talking here about being delivered from sin, but about being delivered from the law.

In this complicated passage in Romans 7, Paul used an analogy. Using the analogy of a woman married to a man, he said, "According to the law, if that woman marries another man while her husband remains alive, she is an adulteress. But once her husband is dead, she's free to marry another man." (See verse 3.) According to Paul, we had been under the law, married to our carnal nature. Out of that union, the carnal nature produced what it always produces—the works of the flesh. Not one good work among them. But Paul conveyed the good news that, on the cross, our carnal nature died in Jesus. Now, we are free to marry "another" without being an adulteress. To whom shall we be married? Christ. If we are married to the resurrected Christ, we will bring forth the fruit of the Spirit. That is what comes out of that union.

There are two possible unions: You can be united with your fleshly nature and bring forth the works of the flesh—marriage under the law. Or, you can be delivered from the law, free to be united by the Holy Spirit to Jesus in a marriage relationship, and bring forth the fruit of the Spirit.

In neither case is it a question of trying or doing our best. Christianity is not a religion of doing our best or a religion of effort. The key word is union. We bring forth what is appropriate to what we unite with. United to our fleshly nature, no matter how hard we try, or how many rules we make, we will bring forth the works of the flesh—not one good work one among them. On the other hand, truly united by the Holy Spirit to Jesus the resurrected Lord, without human effort—we will naturally bring forth the fruit of the Spirit. It is not effort, but union. It is not a new set of rules, but relationship. That principle is so plainly stated in the New Testament that it is amazing the majority of professing Christians have never known it.

Another very simple picture of union is the parable of the vine, which is found in John 15. Jesus said, *"I am the vine, you are the branches. He who abides in Me, and I in him, bears much fruit"* (John 15:5). That's a beautiful parable of the Godhead. Jesus also said, *"My Father is the vinedresser. I am the vine"* (v. 1). Where's the Holy Spirit? He's the sap. The branches do not produce fruit by trying hard, but by abiding in the vine. When they abide in the vine, they can't help but produce fruit. It is not effort, but union.

We see, therefore, that we have been delivered from the law to bring an end to the fleshly activity it produced within us. As Paul said, "Those who are in the flesh cannot please God" (Romans 8:8). On the positive side, we are delivered from the law to be united with Jesus, producing fruit pleasing to God.

Three Freedoms

Let us now examine three key results of being delivered from the Law. First of all, we receive freedom from condemnation.

Freedom from Condemnation

> *There is therefore now no condemnation to those who are in Christ Jesus....For what the law could not do in that it was weak through the flesh, God did by sending His own Son in the likeness of sinful flesh.*
>
> (Romans 8:1, 3)

The book of Romans is like percolated coffee. We know there are two kinds of coffee: percolated and instant. Percolated coffee takes longer because it has to go through the brewing process. Romans is like percolated coffee. We cannot get instant coffee out of Romans 8. We must go through the preceding seven chapters. That is the percolator. But the result is that much richer. Only when we have been through those chapters do we get to the "therefore." The preceding chapters deal with the total sinfulness of all humanity and with the failure of religion to change man's sinful nature. Using the examples of Abraham and David (chapter 4), with a comparison between Adam and Christ (chapter 5), chapter 6 then reveals God's remedy for the old man: execution. God doesn't patch him up. He doesn't reform him. He doesn't send him to church. He executes him! The good news is that this execution took place when Jesus died on the cross.

Romans 7 deals with our relationship to the Law. I always used to think, Why come to the law after all that? But I have learned by my own experience, by dealing with people, and learning from Scripture, that the ultimate hurdle we have to get over (the last stage of this percolator) is how we relate to the law. Most Christians have never gone there. Without the percolator, we cannot live in Romans 8, because the essential condition is *"no condemnation."* The moment we come under condemnation, we are out of the Spirit-controlled life of Romans 8. The devil's number one objective is to bring us under condemnation. The purpose of God's Word, especially in Romans, is to deliver us from condemnation.

Freedom to Love

Second, deliverance from the law brings freedom to love. Just as the law and grace are opposed to each other, so are legalism and love. In a legalistic system, it is very hard to love.

Owe no one anything except to love one another, for he who loves another has fulfilled the Law. (Romans 13:8–10)

Notice that, he who loves "has fulfilled the law." It is not something he yet has to accomplish.

For the commandments, "You shall not commit adultery," "You shall not murder," "You shall not steal," "You shall not bear false witness," "You shall not covet," and if there is any other commandment, are all summed up in this saying, namely, "You shall love your neighbor as yourself." Love does no harm to a neighbor; therefore love is the fulfillment of the law.

(Romans 13:9–10)

That is very simple. In fact, the problem for theologians is that it seems too simple. Yet it is true. Galatians adds this insight:

For in Christ Jesus neither circumcision nor uncircumcision avails anything, but faith working through love.

(Galatians 5:6)

In the last resort, what matters most is faith working through love. If we ever get away from that truth, we have become sidetracked. We can get sidetracked into all sorts of clever theological theories, interpretations, and beliefs. But if we ever get away from faith working through love, we have gone off center. We have missed the central purpose of the gospel message.

For all the law is fulfilled in one word, even in this: "You shall love your neighbor as yourself."　　　　　(v. 14)

Such love is not possible when the law binds us, because we are bound to our carnal nature. As we have seen, the carnal nature produces anything but good fruit.

Freedom to Be Led by the Holy Spirit

The third result of being delivered from the law is freedom to be led by the Holy Spirit.

For as many as are led by the Spirit of God, these are sons of God. For you did not receive the spirit of bondage [slavery] *again to fear, but you received the Spirit of adoption by whom we cry out, "Abba, Father."*   (Romans 8:14–15)

As I have stated before, God has not given us the spirit of slavery, but the spirit of "sonship." God does not want to produce slaves. He wants to produce sons and daughters. The mark of sons of God is stated here very clearly. *"For* as many as are [regularly] *led by the Spirit of God, these are sons of God."*

Most people with a church background have heard sermons on how to be born again, and probably how to be baptized in the Holy Spirit. Those are both tremendous truths. The new birth makes us a child of God. The baptism in the Holy Spirit equips us to serve God with supernatural power. But the only way we can become a mature son of God is by being led by the Holy Spirit.

I have spoken before large congregations and

asked, "How many of you have ever heard a sermon on how to be led by the Holy Spirit?" Very often not more than 25 percent will ever raise their hands, which is a great deficiency. We place all our focus on the one-time experiences and do not realize the importance of the ongoing life in the Spirit.

The words in this verse are in the continuing present. "As many as are being regularly led by the Spirit of God, they [and only they] are sons of God." Put that together with Galatians 5:18 to see the full effect of what I'm trying to share, "But if you are led by the Spirit, you are not under the law."

If we want to be led by the Spirit, we cannot be under the law. And if we are not led by the Spirit, we cannot become mature sons of God. Deliverance from the law means a release to become a mature son or daughter of God through being led by the Holy Spirit. I want to tell you this: the Holy Spirit is a person. He is not a set of rules, nor is He a theological concept. He is not half a sentence at the end of the Apostle's Creed; He is a person. We have to learn to relate to Him as a person and be sensitive to Him.

I realize this is a tremendous problem for religious people. They think, "If I let go of the rules, what will I hold on to? This is dangerous."

Ironically, the Bible tells us what is truly dangerous: to try to live by the rules. There is definitely a place for rules. I believe in keeping the speed limit. I believe in being an obedient citizen of the nation in which we live. I believe there needs to be simple, practical rules for a family. I believe in a few simple principles to guide the conduct of the affairs of the Church. But, we are not made righteous by keeping the rules. If we have been made righteous by faith and the rules are right, we will keep them. But our righteousness does not come from keeping those rules. If the only righteousness we have is keeping rules (which is true of millions of Christians), we have never experienced the righteousness that God intends us to have.

3. DELIVERANCE FROM SELF

I have been crucified with Christ; it is no longer I who live, but Christ lives in me; and the life which I now live in the flesh I live by faith in the Son of God, who loved me and gave Himself for me.
(Galatians 2:20)

It is appropriate that this deliverance is the central one out of five. I don't believe we can ever find the fullness of God's will for our lives or enjoy the full provision of the cross until we allow the cross to put self to death. Self is the root of many evils that are common in the Church: pride, egotism, personal ambition, and sectarianism.

All these represent the uncrucified ego. Racism is another aspect of the uncrucified ego, and we see much racism even in the Christian Church.

When I was pastoring in England in the 1950s, we had a dear "spiritual sister" in our congregation who prayed like an angel for the people of Africa, but when a black brother sat down next to her, it really disturbed her. There is a lot of undercover racism left in some of us, and it is very contrary to the purposes of God for the Church.

Let nothing be done through selfish ambition or conceit, but in lowliness of mind let each esteem others better than himself. (Philippians 2:3)

The attitude described here is the result of the crucifixion of the ego, but it is impossible until we have let our ego die on the cross. Two things that mark the Church very conspicuously are competitiveness and personal ambition. As a minister, I have seen a tremendous amount of personal ambition and competitiveness in Christian ministry today. The cause? Our egos have not been dealt with on the cross.

I will now point out the real dividing line between the true Church and the world today. In 2 Timothy, Paul gave us a very vivid description of the degeneration of human character that will mark the close of this age. How many of these eighteen moral and ethical blemishes are conspicuous in our current society?

> *But know this, that in the last days perilous times will come: For men will be lovers of themselves, lovers of money, boasters, proud, blasphemers, disobedient to parents, unthankful, unholy, unloving, unforgiving, slanderers, without self-control, brutal, despisers of good, traitors, headstrong, haughty, lovers of pleasures rather than lovers of God.*
>
> (2 Timothy 3:1–4)

You might say, "This is a terrible list, but at least we don't find these blemishes in the Church." That is a huge mistake, because the next verse says:

> *...having a form of godliness...*   (v. 5)

I don't believe Paul would have ever used the word *godliness* in relation to a religion that had nothing to do with the Bible or with Jesus Christ. These are people who have made some kind of profession of church membership. But Paul went on to say:

...denying its power.   (v. 5)

These who deny the power of godliness to radically change human nature are religious, but they just go on living the same kind of life that they lived before they professed religion. The list above begins and ends with what people love. The first item in the list is lovers of themselves, the next is lovers of money, and the last is lovers of pleasure.

Let's consider those three characteristics for a moment—love of self, love of money, love of pleasure. They are probably the three most characteristic features of our contemporary culture, and I would quickly add that the root of all is the first one—love of self. The mere fact that people don't swear, gamble, or use alcohol, tobacco, or drugs doesn't necessarily indicate that they are Christians. We can't base our claim to being a Christian on the fact that we don't do these obvious sins because, for example, we might still be very selfish. The real distinguishing line between the world and the true Church is whether people are lovers of self or whether self has been crucified and they are living for something other than themselves.

We often hear this parody of the typical prayer of the average church member. "God bless me and my wife, my son, John, and his wife, us four, no more. Amen."

That is religious, but extremely selfish, isn't it? How many of us are self-centered in our prayers? How many of us ever pray beyond a little narrow circle of the things that interest me and concern me? But God has provided a way of release from this focus. It comes through the cross. We can make this decision and affirmation, "I have been crucified with Christ; it is no longer I who live, but Christ lives in me."

That step requires two actions: first of all, a decision, and second, the right confession. It is important to make a personal confession. In Romans 6, Paul said,

"Our old man was crucified with Him" (verse 6). That is a general statement. But in Galatians 2:20, Paul made it his personal testimony: "I have been crucified with Christ; it is no longer I who live, but Christ lives in me."

The Crucified Ego

There are three direct results of the crucified ego in our lives. First of all, there is the freedom to serve.

Freedom to Serve

> *Jesus called them* [His disciples] *to Himself and said to them, "You know that those who are considered rulers over the Gentiles lord it over them, and their great ones exercise authority over them. Yet it shall not be so among you; but whoever desires to become great among you shall be your servant. And whoever of you desires to be first shall be slave of all."*
>
> (Mark 10:42–44)

Several years ago a young man came to me who was a committed Christian, a man with considerable gifts. He said to me, "Brother Prince, I want to serve you." Well, that wasn't altogether good news to me because I'm a very self-sufficient person. I thought, *I'm really getting along all right without you. If you start serving me, I'm going to have you on the scene at a lot of times when I'd rather be on my own. And, you're going to be observing me in situations when I might not wish to be observed.* So I said, "I'll think it over." But when I prayed, the Lord said, "If you don't give that young man an opportunity to serve you, you shut the only door to legitimate promotion." So I told the young man, "Okay." And we built a wonderful relationship, and God steadily promoted him in the kingdom. What a great lesson that was for me.

Promotion doesn't come from man; it comes from God. Jesus said that if we want to be great, we have to become a servant. If we want to be the master, we have to become the slave. In other words, the higher up you want to go, the lower down you have to start. Once again, consider the words of Jesus in Matthew 23:12 (also Luke 14:11), *"For whoever exalts himself will be humbled, and he who humbles himself will be exalted."* That's a rule that governs the universe. Do you want promotion? I can guarantee it to you. Just humble yourself and submit to a low place.

Find somewhere or someone to serve. But you won't be able to do that as long as the ego in you has not been dealt with. The uncrucified ego corrupts service.

The path to authority and leadership in the Church is through serving. There is no other legitimate way. Anyone who comes to a position of authority in the Church by any other path will not be able to exercise authority rightly.

Freedom from Self-effort

The second result of the crucified ego is freedom from self-effort and self-promotion. What a glorious deliverance!

> *For we do not preach ourselves, but Christ Jesus the Lord, and ourselves your servants* ["slaves" in Greek] *for Jesus' sake.* (2 Corinthians 4:5)

That is a remarkable statement at any time, but when we consider who made it to whom, it is much more remarkable. Consider the very self-righteous Pharisee, Saul of Tarsus, who had been brought up to believe that he and his nation were the only chosen ones. Paul had been taught to live a certain kind of very strict life and observe a whole lot of regulations. Otherwise, he would be impure and unclean. Paul even referred to Gentiles as dogs. Then he met Jesus on the Damascus road, and Jesus changed him!

We find Saul some years later writing to the believers in Corinth, a wicked seaport. The list of what these people were doing is somewhat shocking. They were prostitutes, pimps, homosexuals, drunkards; every kind of vile sin had been practiced among them. But they had been gloriously changed by the power of the gospel!

Now consider what it meant for Paul to write to those people and say, "We're not preaching ourselves, but we're preaching Jesus Christ the Lord, and ourselves your slaves for Jesus' sake." That is the crucified ego!

In 1957, I went to Kenya in East Africa for five years to train African teachers for African schools. I don't consider myself a racially prejudiced person. After all, at that time I had eight adopted daughters of whom six were Jewish, one was Arab, and one was English. But, when I came to that situation and I really wanted God to have His way, I had to decide for myself who I really was. I was a graduate of Cambridge. I was a scholar of Eton. From the point of view of the academic life of Britain, I had reached the pinnacle. All of my ancestors had been officers in the British army. I really had to ask myself, "Am I willing to say to these black students, 'Not me, but Jesus Christ the Lord; and I'm your servant'?" Thankfully, I can say, to the glory of God, I did it joyfully. And I was never happier in ministry than I was in East Africa.

Freedom from Justifying Myself

Finally, the last result of crucifying the ego is that I don't need to prove myself right. Oh, what a relief! What a blessing! People can disagree with me and argue with me. But I can say, "Let's wait and see who's right. I could be wrong." That's amazing, isn't it? A preacher could be wrong! What a burden was lifted from me when I discovered I didn't have to justify myself.

4. DELIVERANCE FROM THE FLESH

*And those who are Christ's have crucified
the flesh with its passions and desires.*
(Galatians 5:24)

The mark that we belong to Jesus Christ is that we have crucified the flesh. That is the evidence. "Those who are Christ's have crucified the flesh."

In 1 Corinthians 15:23, Paul told us that when Jesus comes back, He is coming back for those who are His. This verse in Galatians tells us that those who are His are those who have crucified the flesh with its affections and desires. Who is Jesus coming back for? Those who have crucified the flesh. He is not coming back for everybody who professes to be a Christian and leads a carnal, selfish, self-indulgent life. He is coming back for those who have allowed the cross to do its work in their carnal nature.

> *For the flesh lusts against the Spirit, and the Spirit against the flesh; and these are contrary to one another, so that you do not do the things that you wish.*
>
> (Galatians 5:17)

Before God changes our fleshly nature, it is in total opposition to the Spirit of God.

> *So then, those who are in the flesh cannot please God.*   (Romans 8:8)

Those who are living according to their old carnal, unregenerate nature cannot please God. Whether they are religious or unreligious is not important.

> *Therefore, brethren, we are debtors; not to the flesh, to live according to the flesh. For if you live according to the flesh you will die; but if by the Spirit you put to death the deeds of the body, you will live.*
>
> (Romans 8:12–13)

It is our responsibility to put to death the deeds of the flesh. Christ has made it possible, but we have to apply it.

Consider for a moment what is covered by the flesh. It is not just immorality, as some might assume. In fact, that is not really the main expression of the flesh. Fear, resentment, anger, greed, covetousness, sexual lusts, and fluctuating moods are all common manifestations of the fleshly nature. A moody Christian, first of all, reflects a denial of the faith. Second, he or she is evidence that the flesh has not been crucified. By the grace of God, I can say I am not a moody person today, because I have allowed the cross to do its work in me and deal with my moods. We must understand that the flesh wars against the Spirit, and the Spirit against the flesh.

5. DELIVERANCE FROM THE WORLD

But God forbid that I should glory except in the cross of our Lord Jesus Christ, by whom [or by which] *the world has been crucified to me, and I to the world.*

(Galatians 6:14)

The cross separates us and releases us from a society that is not subject to the righteous government of God. Jesus said, "You aren't in the world because I called you out of the world." This does not mean that God asks us to close our eyes and ears and walk around as though the physical, material world around us does not exist. There is one simple way to be separated from the world. It is to be totally committed to the government of Jesus in our lives. That is what the world is not.

When we look at the world now, between the world and us is a corpse hanging on a cross, and when the world looks at us, it sees the same thing. There is a complete separation. It is not physical, but it is in the spiritual realm. We belong to a totally different realm. We are released from the world's opinions, values, judgments, pressures, enticements, and deceptions—the present world order which is controlled by Satan.

> *The whole world lies under the sway of the*
> *wicked one.*   (1 John 5:19)

> *The great dragon...that serpent of old...the*
> *Devil and Satan, who deceives the whole*
> *world.*   (Revelation 12:9)

Once Christians begin to come under the influence of the world, they come under deception, because the Spirit of God and the spirit of this world are opposites.

Now we have received, not the spirit of the world, but the Spirit who is from God, that we might know the things that have been freely given to us by God.

(1 Corinthians 2:12)

Results of Deliverance from the World

The spirit of this world will obscure all that has been given to us by God. The Spirit of God will reveal all He has given us.

Commitment to Christ's Kingdom

The first result of being delivered from the world is commitment to Christ's kingdom.

But seek first the kingdom of God and His righteousness; and all these things shall be added to you. (Matthew 6:33)

I have not been totally faithful to God as I would have wished. But looking back, I would have to say I have proved that Scripture to be effective in my own experience over many years. It is true. It works.

Freedom from Satan's Manipulation

Second, you are free from Satan's manipulations and deceptions. That is true, especially today, in regards to the media. This freedom is tremendously important because our minds are being continuously bombarded with presentations, most of which are false. In the truest sense, they are spiritually untrue.

Freedom to Refuse to Bow

Finally, release from the dominion of this world means that we will have the power—like Shadrach, Meshach, and Abednego (see Daniel 3:1-26)—to refuse to bow before the world's idols. The pressure is tremendous, especially among young people today, to bow before the world's idols. These include worldly success, popularity, wealth, power, pleasure, and comfort.

Some solemn words in the book of Hebrews will both encourage and challenge us:

> *So do not throw away your confidence; it will be richly rewarded. You need to persevere so that when you have done the will of God, you will receive what He has promised. For in just a very little while,*

"He who is coming will come and will not delay. But my righteous one will live by faith. And if he shrinks back, I will not be pleased with him." But we are not of those who shrink back and are destroyed, but of those who believe and are saved.

(Hebrews 10:35–39 NIV)

I see three main warnings in that passage. First, we must not throw away our confidence. For those of us who have a strong faith, we must be careful not to give up the good we have received from God.

Second, perseverance is needed to obtain the promises of God. It is one thing to fulfill the conditions; it is another to receive the promise. Almost all of us know from experience that there is often a considerable interval of time between our doing what entitles us to the promise and our receiving the fulfillment of the promise. In that interval, we have to practice perseverance.

Third, we must remember the reward is ahead. It is when He who is coming will come. That is when the final reward comes. We have to persevere until then. This passage really leaves us with only two alternatives: we either persevere, or we shrink back. If we persevere, we will inherit the promise. But if we shrink back, we will be destroyed. That is very strong language. But I am grateful for the honesty of the Word of God that confronts us so frankly. Which are we going to do? Are we going to persevere? Or are we going to shrink back?

Our Call to Battle

You are in a battle against an invisible enemy in their invisible kingdom that will use witchcraft in an attempt to destroy mankind—the image of God. Through pride and guilt, Satan attempts to subvert what God has created. Thankfully, God was willing to stoop down and redeem creation through the one-time sacrifice of His Son, Jesus Christ. Through His death, Jesus disarmed the principalities and powers of Satan, forever extinguishing the guilt and sin that separated you from God.

Paul said that sin will no longer have dominion over you because you are no longer under the law but under grace.

For Christ is the end of the law for righteousness to every one who believes.
(Romans 10:4)

Do you believe? Then Christ is the end of the law for righteousness to you. Not the end of the law as part of God's Word, not the end of the law as part of the history of the culture of Israel; but the end of the law as a means of achieving righteousness with God. That's it for everyone who believes, Jew or Gentile, Protestant or Catholic. If you want to be reckoned righteous with God by the death of Jesus on the cross, it means the end of the law.

And it is that work of the cross that continues to enforce Christ's victory over Satan today. It is the only way out of the evil of this age and the pressures placed upon us by the current society of this world.

But we must apply it daily to receive our full deliverance. You can apply the cross in your life. You can be delivered from this evil age—from the law, from self, from the flesh, and from the world.

You can disarm Satan. And when you disarm the enemy using the cross as your weapon, you will find a place of ultimate security—a place on the other side of the cross. That security comes as we make a commitment to God to go His way. It comes as we deny ourselves, take up our cross, and follow Him.

Will you commit yourself to do what Jesus said? Deny yourself. Take up your cross. Follow Him!

[1] See 1 Chronicles 29:10; Nehemiah 9:5; Psalm 9:5; 10:16; 21:4; 45:6, 17; 48:14; 52:8; 111:8; 119:44; 145:1–2, 21; 148:6; Isaiah 30:8; 45:17; Jeremiah 7:7; 25:5; Daniel 2:20; 12:3; Micah 4:5; Galatians 1:5; Ephesians 3:21; Philippians 4:20; 1 Timothy 1:17; 2 Timothy 4:18; Hebrews 1:8; 13:21; 1 Peter 4:11; 5:11; Revelation 1:6; 4:9–10; 5:13–14; 7:12; 10:6; 11:15; 14:11; 15:7; 19:3; 20:10; and 22:5.

DEREK PRINCE

1915 – 2003

Derek Prince (1915–2003) was born in India of British parents. Educated as a scholar of Greek and Latin at Eton College and Cambridge University, England, he held a Fellowship in Ancient and Modern Philosophy at King's College. He also studied several modern languages, including Hebrew and Aramaic, at Cambridge University and the Hebrew University in Jerusalem.

While serving with the British army in World War II, he began to study the Bible and experienced a life-changing encounter with Jesus Christ. Out of this encounter he formed two conclusions: first, that Jesus Christ is alive; second, that the Bible is a true, relevant, up-to-date book. These conclusions altered the whole course of his life, which he then devoted to studying and teaching the Bible.

Derek's main gift of explaining the Bible and its teaching in a clear and simple way has helped build a foundation of faith in millions of lives. His non-denominational, non-sectarian approach has made his teaching equally relevant and helpful to people from all racial and religious backgrounds.

He is the author of over 50 books, 600 audio and 100 video teachings, many of which have been translated and published in more than 100 languages. His daily radio broadcast is translated into Arabic, Chinese (Amoy, Cantonese,Mandarin, Shanghainese, Swatow), Croatian, German, Malagasy, Mongolian, Russian, Samoan, Spanish and Tongan. The radio program continues to touch lives around the world.

Derek Prince Ministries continues to reach out to believers in over 140 countries with Derek's teachings, fulfilling the mandate to keep on "until Jesus returns". This is effected through the outreaches of more than 30 Derek Prince Offices around the world, including primary work in Australia, Canada, China, France, Germany, the Netherlands, New Zealand, Norway, Russia, South Africa, Switzerland, the United Kingdom and the United States. For current information about these and other worldwide locations, visit www.derekprince.com

BOOKS BY DEREK PRINCE

Promise of Provision, The
Prophetic Guide to the End
    Times
Protection from Deception
Pulling Down Strongholds
Receiving God's Best
Rediscovering God's Church
Resurrection of the Body *
Rules of Engagement
Secrets of a Prayer Warrior
Self-Study Bible Course
    (revised and expanded)
Set Apart For God
Shaping History Through Prayer
    and Fasting
Spiritual Warfare
Surviving the Last Days

Thanksgiving, Praise and
    Worship
They Shall Expel Demons
Three Most Powerful Words, The
Through Repentance to Faith *
Through the Psalms with
    Derek Prince
Transmitting God's Power *
The Two Harvests
Three Messages For Israel
War in Heaven
Where Wisdom Begins
Who Is the Holy Spirit?
Will You Intercede?
You Matter to God
You Shall Receive Power

Get the Complete Laying the Foundations Series*

1. Founded on the Rock (B100)
2. Authority and Power of God's Word (B101)
3. Through Repentance to Faith (B102)
4. Faith and Works (B103)
5. The Doctrine of Baptisms (B104)
6. Immersion in The Spirit (B105)
7. Transmitting God's Power (B106)
8. At the End of Time (B107)
9. Resurrection of the Body (B108)
10. Final Judgment (B109)

DEREK PRINCE MINISTRIES
WWW.DEREKPRINCE.COM

DEREK PRINCE MINISTRIES OFFICES WORLDWIDE

DPM–Asia/Pacific
38 Hawdon Street, Sydenham
Christchurch 8023,
New Zealand
T: + 64 3 366 4443
E: admin@dpm.co.nz
W: www.dpm.co.nz and
www.derekprince.in

DPM–Australia
Unit 21/317-321
Woodpark Road, Smithfield
New South Wales 2165,
Australia
T: + 612 9604 0670
E: enquiries@derekprince.com.au
W: www.derekprince.com.au

DPM–Canada
P. O. Box 8354 Halifax,
Nova Scotia B3K 5M1,
Canada
T: + 1 902 443 9577
E: enquiries.dpm@eastlink.ca
W: www.derekprince.org

DPM–France
B.P. 31, 9, Route d'Oupia,
34210 Olonzac,
France
T: + 33 468 913872
E: info@derekprince.fr
W: www.derekprince.fr

DPM–Germany
Söldenhofstr. 10
D-83308 Trostberg,
Germany
T: + 49 8621 64146
E: IBL.de@t-online.de
W: www.ibl-dpm.net

DPM–Nederland
Postbus 326
7100 VB
Winterswijk
Phone: (+31) 251-255044
E: info@dpmnederland.nl
W: www.derekprince.nl

DPM–Norway
P. O. Box 129
Lodderfjord
N-5881, Bergen,
Norway
T: +47 928 39855
E: sverre@derekprince.no
W: www.derekprince.no

Derek Prince Publications Pte. Ltd.
P. O. Box 2046 ,
Robinson Road Post Office
Singapore 904046
T: + 65 6392 1812
E: dpmchina@singnet.com.sg
English web: www.dpmchina.org
Chinese web: www.ygmweb.org

DPM–South Africa
P. O. Box 33367
Glenstantia 0010 Pretoria
South Africa
T: +27 12 348 9537
E: enquiries@derekprince.co.za
W: www.derekprince.co.za

DPM–Switzerland
Alpenblick 8
CH-8934 Knonau
Switzerland
T: + 41(0) 44 768 25 06
E: dpm-ch@ibl-dpm.net
W: www.ibl-dpm.net

DPM–UK
PO Box 393
HITCHIN
SG5 9EU
UK
T: + 44 (0) 1462 492100
E: enquiries@dpmuk.org
W: www.dpmuk.org

DPM–USA
P. O. Box 19501
Charlotte NC 28219,
USA
T: + 1 704 357 3556
E: ContactUs@derekprince.org
W: www.derekprince.org

CPSIA information can be obtained
at www.ICGtesting.com
Printed in the USA
LVHW081617020623
748743LV00009B/1120

9 781782 633341